Embracing Goodness

How Life Works

Jon Edward Gauthier

Gotham Books
30 N Gould St.
Ste. 20820, Sheridan, WY 82801
https://gothambooksinc.com/
Phone: 1 (307) 464-7800

Published by Gotham Books (June 2022)

ISBN: Paperback   978-1-956349-68-9
                   eBook   978-1-956349-69-6

Because of the dynamic nature of the Internet, any web addresses or links contained in this book may have changed since publication and may no longer be valid.

The views expressed in this work are solely those of the author and do not necessarily reflect the views of the publisher, and the publisher hereby disclaims any responsibility for them.

Cover photograph by Melissa Gauthier.

Dedicated to St. Thérèse of Lisieux,
Through whom the Holy Spirit communicated to me the inspiration
To write this book;

To my wife, Mary Anne, who I love more every day;

To my daughters, Laura and Melissa, and son, Jon Philip,
To whom I offer my simple perceptions of Truth
To guide them in Life;

And finally, to my siblings and parents, living and deceased,
Whose palpable spirits reside in my soul always.

—Jon Gauthier

Contents

Note from the Author:

It has now been over twenty years since I wrote the first chapters for this book, and over ten years since its original publication. While it is an imperfect attempt to explain how the goodness of the Lord works, it has been for me a major part of discovering God's love.

Do I have a mission? Yes, to save souls, including my own. I strive to communicate that life is simple because the fundamentals upon which everything is based are simple. *If this book is complex, I've lost touch with how life works.*

I also set out to be concise. The fewer the pages, the more it would be understood. (And of course, the fewer the pages, the more I would understand it!)

And while there is nothing "new" in this book, I hope there is a greater clarity to what you already know and perhaps have forgotten.

It is especially written for my children: *Laura, with your very bright intelligence, you will benefit greatly from literal directions; Melissa, you are naturally good, but you will benefit greatly from understanding temptation and how to avoid it; and Jon Philip, with your very strong will, you will benefit greatly from understanding how you must bend your will in order to do God's will. Each of you will benefit in unique ways, but also in shared ways.*

The book is primarily an attempt for understanding "how" life works. It is not a book about "why." Only God can answer that. Occasionally we are partly given revelations of "why" certain things happen, from our understanding of each individual's use of free will to seeing a glimpse of God's love intervening in our lives as a result of prayer. But we can never fully understand "why" until we meet God face-to-face, hopefully as we join Him in heaven. Until then, we can learn *"how life works"* and live our lives to the fullest of joy in God's love.

The inspiration and obligation to write this book came while reading *"The Story of a Soul,"* the autobiography of St. Thérèse of Lisieux. *To me, the miracle of St. Thérèse's book is the sustained state of grace she maintained while writing it.* And although I am certainly not worthy to have learned so much so quickly, I allowed myself to approximate her sustained state of grace by reading it—and I encourage you to read it as well. Subsequently, the text of *Embracing Goodness* is focused on the application of the principles of St. Therese's book in a modern world. She did little things with great love. *This book is about avoiding your threshold of temptation and embracing goodness, wherever it is*—even if it is in those who have sinned against us, or sinned against someone we love. I only pray that I am doing His will.

Early on, I asked, "How should I write this book? What is my outline?" I prayed for guidance. In my heart, I received an answer: Parables. Later, feeling burdened with the weight of covering too much and possibly forgetting something important, God answered my prayers again: Do not burden yourself with everything; and do not fear imperfection. *Just as no one can make another believe before they are ready, so too, you cannot pretend to have perfect knowledge when you are still on the path to discovering Truth.*

The parables in this book are based on real stories I have experienced or learned from others. While some of them are unique, others are based on multiple experiences of the same story. Any errors in summarizing these stories are my own.

The impact of this book is significant—if for no other reason than *it has changed how I live my life.* I pray that it will have a positive impact on you. A passage from the *"Story of a Soul"* stands out in my mind. St. Thérèse writes: "I felt it better to speak to God than about him. There's often so much self-love involved in the chatter about spiritual things." I hope that I have not failed this test. While writing this book, whenever self-pride got in the way, the words were long and confusing. When I simply let the Holy Spirit take over, the words were brief and direct.

I would not have been able to write this book without the love of my wife, children, parents, in-laws, siblings, friends, and others. To each of them, I owe an eternal debt of gratitude.

While writing this book, the working title was "How Life Works." Over time, I realized this did not communicate *the actions* we must take when we begin to understand *how life works,* and thus the title, *"Embracing Goodness." Even though He allows us to reject Him, He waits for us to embrace Him, to embrace His love, every day.*

Introduction

Over the course of life, we see first-hand the miracles of life and discover its revelations. We were not created as a mistake or a random evolution, but in the image of God.

The purpose of this book is to focus on the fundamentals of life, and how we are to live it. Not a book with a beginning, middle, and end, it is a collection of principles and guiding insights and is best read in its entirety, especially as it relates to free will and the timelessness of heaven, although it can also be read in parts.

The last pages, entitled "Remembering Miracles and Revelations," begins with a few examples of miracles and revelations that I have witnessed or learned of, but the rest of it is left blank for you to write down your own. I strongly encourage you to use this section or begin your own book of miracles and revelations to capture your glimpses of Truth and to help you recall the little things that reveal our faith.

The closer I am to God the less it is me who writes these words. So I pray that you will overlook my shortcomings, read further, and achieve a state of grace that can only come from God. If you choose not to read further, simply take away these words: "to love God with all your heart and soul and mind and to treat others as yourselves." The second part of that sentence, known as the "Golden Rule," is almost universally accepted in the free world. *The first part, which encompasses a rejection of self-love and an acceptance of God, is the most difficult to embrace and the cause for so much misunderstanding. In its most basic form, it requires one to be thankful to God. With time, one can give thanks and praise.*

St. Thérèse of Lisieux lived by these words in the purest of Truth. She not only loved God with all her heart, soul, and mind, and loved others as herself, she also embraced Jesus' New Commandment, "To love one another as I have loved you."

She is remembered for doing little things with great love. My hope is that you will learn to avoid temptation and embrace goodness wherever you find it.

Enjoy this book. I learned as much by writing it as I hope you will by reading it.

Chapter 1

Life Changing Events

In every person's life, there are events that change how they think, what they feel, and even who they are. For me, it began when I was 12 years old. I grew up in a large family, the seventh child and third son of 15 children. As you might expect, we were a bunch of kids at an endless party. But how little we knew.

On a fall October night in 1975, my older brother Tom died in a motorcycle accident. In 1977, my older sister Kathy died in a car accident. Two years after that, in 1979, I lost three sisters—my older sister Jackie and two younger sisters, Mickey and Kelly—and a young cousin, Trista, in another car accident. Our lives screeched to a halt. How could God allow this?

My experience is that it takes three years after a traumatic event to find what I call a "new normal." Your heart aches and your mind races endlessly to re-create the events to somehow undo them, but you can't.

People ask, "How do you survive?" Numb then and calmly now, I can only say, "Do you have a choice?" *We moved forward because it was our condition to live—even if painfully.*

To others, I would simply say the question is not whether a life-changing event will occur, but when. I'm always amazed at the number of people who say they have never suffered the loss of a loved one or another kind of tragedy before it happens. *I have come to understand that everyone will suffer life changing events in their lifetime—everyone.*

Life changing events not only can happen—they will happen. Prepare your heart and soul by cherishing the people in your life, accepting the world as fragile, and living your life focused on eternity.

Thomas "Tom" Dominic Gauthier: Born August 30, 1959; deceased October 9, 1975.

Kathleen "Kathy" Louise Gauthier: Born June 6, 1958; deceased August 26, 1977.

Jacqueline "Jackie" Erma Gauthier: Born December 26, 1960; deceased June 15, 1979.

Michelle "Mickey" Lucille Gauthier: Born February 20, 1969; deceased, June 15, 1979.

Kelly "Kelly" Sue Gauthier: Born October 10, 1970; deceased, June 15, 1979.

Trista "Trista" Danielle Hawkins: Born May 27, 1971; deceased, June 15, 1979.

Chapter 2

Believing in God

Believing in God is simply being perceptive to the world around you—and seeing how things work. He speaks clearly in times of trouble, and He speaks clearly when we nurture peace in our hearts—cultivating it in our minds and in our lives. But he is always communicating:

— It is seeing a baby come into the world, holding him in your arms for the first time, and *understanding for an instant that God is real*;
— It is traveling a dangerous road, feeling the car weave beneath you in the rain or on the snow, and *knowing that God's grace is keeping you from harm*;
— It is welcoming a pet into the family and *learning first-hand what unconditional love is*;
— It is seeing the sunset or sunrise from a mountaintop or over the ocean and *glimpsing the power and glory of God—even if it changes before your eyes and slips away*; and,
— It is praying for peace in a hostile world and *knowing in your heart that it is through prayer and divine intervention in combination with man's will, and not simply man's will, that keeps us from crossing the brink of disaster.*

In all these ways, God is around us, available for us to perceive Him—present to carry us in our moments of weakness. *All we must do is look for him, ask for His help through prayer, and seek and do His will.* (Remember, "Seek and ye shall find.")

Chapter 3

Sadness and the Happy Warrior

Many years ago, I met a woman who grew sad because of the many injustices in the world. When at first she saw prejudice, poverty, and the lack of human dignity between people she became angry. When nothing changed, she grew sad.

Her sadness grew. It began to overwhelm her so that she told her colleagues it was "sad" to see all the things that were wrong in the world—things that should not be.

Over time, she knew how God expected her to help. *Simply feeling sad over life's injustices was useless. Instead, she understood that God intended for her to help. In a divine way, beyond her complete comprehension, she understood that these injustices were permitted to draw her closer to God—and to draw others closer to God.*

In the end, God would enable good to overcome evil. But she needed to choose to help if it were to happen sooner.

In a homily years ago, I listened as a priest described hope as having two daughters, anger and courage: 1) Anger because what is, *should not be*; and, 2) courage because what is not, *should be*. I thought of the woman I knew; if you do not react to anger with courage, it is likely nothing will happen and you will grow sad. *Before feeling sad again she would remember her role to act with courage.* From then on, she would be the happy warrior.

More and more, as she sought to do His will, she would work and not grow weary.

Chapter 4

Living My Life With *More Than* the One Rule: To Treat Others the Way I Want To Be Treated

One evening, in conversation with a well-educated woman, it became apparent that she doubted the existence of God. She asked, "How could God allow so much evil in the world? For example, how could He allow the *Shoah*, or Holocaust, to happen?"

Recently, she had lost a brother to cancer who was only in his 30s. She and her family had prayed for his recovery without success. Now, she felt a deep anger with God. She asked, "If he exists, where is He?"

She said she *'wanted'* to believe in God, but how could she? Without believing in God, she decided to anchor her life with one rule: "to treat others the way she wanted to be treated." And yet, occasionally, she had glimpses that something was wrong with her view of the world. Sometimes she felt *"thankful"* for her husband, her family, and her beautiful surroundings—but to whom?

She had been seeing only one-half of how life works, and not the other. If you were to go to a friend's house and have dinner and leave without saying "thank you," how would your friend feel? Your friend would be hurt. For God, it would not be right. *For us not to give thanks is for us not to return God's love with love.*

She still resisted. She asked, "Isn't His love unconditional? Why would He care if we were not thankful? Does it really matter?"

Jesus taught us how to answer these and similar questions when he spoke of the Ten Commandments and gave us the Great Commandment, based on two principles: *1) Give thanks and praise to God, loving him with all your heart, soul, and mind, and honor no other God before him; and, 2) do unto others as you would have them do unto you.* After his death and resurrection, Jesus gave us even more specific guidance, the New Commandment, *"To love one another as I have loved you."*

She was halfway there, and as we spoke, she began to see clearly the other half of her journey. *She opened herself to the concept that you must do more than treat others the way you want to be treated—you must love God.* And to love God, you must be willing to do it as Jesus had done, by serving others. Jesus gave to us even though we could never repay him. Ultimately, He gave his life for us so that we might live.

In a tearful revelation, she knew God existed—even if he allowed bad things to happen.

Chapter 5

Pride

Many years ago, I knew a man who wanted to change the world—to help those who didn't know that someone cared—and saw how technology could improve their lives.

He worked day and night, toiling to get closer to perfection. And yet, in his heart, he knew the pride he took in his life's work was hollow. In the end, how could he take credit for what he'd done? Was it not his friends who encouraged him? His parents who raised him? His financial supporters who believed in him when others did not? Surely, all of these others deserved credit. He generously gave credit to the others. But they could not accept his credit—just as surely as he could not accept theirs.

Over time, he understood.

He knew but had not fully embraced that though we are many parts, we are all one body. *Just as the body cannot be made up of all hands or eyes, so it is that an individual cannot perform the duties of everyone else. We need each other as sure as the hand needs the eye and the eye needs the hand. We make up one body—just as God intended.*

He also read a passage written by Saint Thérèse of Lisieux, the "Little Flower," and the person whom Mother Teresa modeled her life after:

"When I say that all praise leaves me unmoved, I'm not thinking of the love and confidence you show me. I'm very moved by it, but I feel that I can now need have no fear of praise and that I can accept it calmly. For I attribute to God all the goodness with which he has endowed me. It is nothing to do with me if it pleases him to make me seem better than I am." *

---

* *"The Autobiography of a Soul"* by St. Thérèse of Lisieux.

The man now understood that pride can be an evil force, such as self-pride, because it is wrongly placed. But pride in the goodness of the Lord is well placed, "from whom all good things come."

Chapter 6

The Human Condition to Forget

One of the human conditions is to forget. It is one of the reasons why we need to write things down. It is also why I needed to write this book—to help me remember what I have learned.

We need to refresh our memories. We need to talk with others. We need to go to church.

If we don't learn from our mistakes, we will repeat them. And yet, why must we make our own mistakes time and time again? On everything?

God intends for us to remember. He gave Moses the Ten Commandments to guide us in life so we would not make the same mistakes as those before him. He sent us His only Son to save us from sin and clarify The Way, The Truth, and The Light. He would not have done these things if He intended for us to forget.

The prophets and disciples shared their words with others in what would become the Old and New Testaments—these things were done to help us remember and overcome our condition to forget. God has given us the knowledge we need—we need to choose to work to remember—and use it.

Chapter 7

Free Will

How do you choose to use your free will? Do you bend it to God's will? Or is it simply your own?

The least understood aspect of how life works is free will. This may be because of a conflict that we have that while our free will impacts the world around us, there remains a deep-rooted sense among many that they have a "fate" or "destiny" that will occur despite any action they take. This is wrong. *It is the intertwining of man's free will and God's will that create the events of history.* Fate and destiny are created only after the use of our free will. Pope John Paul II observed, "History is not a meaningless series of events, but is the path humanity travels toward God."* Free will matters.

Pope John Paul II goes on to say that God desires each of us to reach the ultimate goal where "God will be all in all."* Our decisions impact when and which of us will share in that glory.

A child may ask, "If you had to choose between red and blue, would God know which color you would choose?" In heaven, where time does not exist as on earth, God is omniscient and thus always knows which color you will choose. But in his love for us, He also allows man to co-author history, and thus even though He knows what we will choose, He allows the choice to be ours. God knows us so well that He knows which one we *should* choose—the one that would be better for us—because He knows what we need even before we ask. *But He still allows us to choose.*

God is always communicating with us and hoping that we will love Him. Thus, He is always giving us opportunities to change the course of history—and it can be a positive change, if we will only choose to love

Him. God is communicating with us to *change history*, even though at every instant he knows what will happen. *In this way, God made us in His image and gave us free will that allows us to choose between Good and Evil—even free will to choose between colors.*

The most famous—or infamous—use of man's free will is Adam and Eve's decision to eat the apple. God admonished them not to but they disobeyed God. God even promised to give them everything they would need if they would not, but they were fooled into believing that they could not trust him. Instead, they believed they could be just like him—if only they tasted the fruit of knowledge.

Adam and Eve committed the first sin—a sin that still separates us from God. We have been seeking reconciliation ever since. And yet, as Pope John Paul II has said, "God the Father is not in any way indifferent to the things that happen to us. The depth of God's love is fully revealed"* when he sent His only Son, Jesus, into the world.

In prayerful use of our free will, prayer to have the wisdom to seek God's will, prayer to have the patience to find it, and prayer to have the courage to act on God's revelations to us, we can alter the course of history to lessen hardship and grow in love.

The presence of free will does not mean that fate and destiny do not exist. To the contrary, one must continually choose the use of his or her own free will. *If you seek His will and act to do his will, your destiny will be eternal life. If you reject His will and act against it, your fate will be unending death.* In this sense, it is man's free will that creates fate and destiny. And man's fate or destiny will only be determined after he chooses the use of his own free will.

---

* From Pope John Paul II's weekly Wednesday addresses as reported in *The Catholic News and Herald.*

Chapter 8

Free Will and Its Impact On Others

Is it not true that you, or I, or anyone else, could wake up in the morning and choose to use their free will to do evil to another? Of course. Would this be God's will? No. God gave us free will in His image, but it's still *free will*.

In using free will, we have a choice. We can bend it to God's will, or we can selfishly keep it our own.

When others choose to use their free will in a way that is harmful to others, we have an obligation to God to use our free will to soften their blows, counter their attacks, and stop evil. When we pray to God, we are asking for his divine intervention to guide, supersede or supplement our own or others' free will.

Actions *and prayers* both matter. *One cannot do God's will without the other. And it is always better to pray before taking action—even though prayer is so powerful it can have an impact after actions.*

And the use of our free will impacts others.

Chapter 9

The Holy Spirit

Three children were playing when they became involved in the discussion of the Holy Spirit. If the Holy Spirit is inside them, why do they bother to go to church, learn about the Bible, or pray? Isn't this enough?

They asked the father of another who told them, "Yes, you have the Holy Spirit within you. It is with you in times of trouble, in moments of glory, and throughout your day. You do not have to seek it because it is within you and simply must be found.

"But the Holy Spirit is also present in those around you, those who have reached a greater understanding of love and peace and joy, and you can learn from them to help you find the depths of the Holy Spirit in your heart.

"Also, you'll find that the Holy Spirit fills your heart with the right guidance, just in time. Sometimes before tragedy to help you avoid it, sometimes to fill your heart with understanding just after you experience tragedy, to help you cope and survive.

"You see, the Holy Spirit is in each one of us, and we cannot shut out others without losing the ability to fully understand ourselves.

"Go now, play and enjoy yourselves, but listen to your friends, expand your heart, and prepare yourselves for life's many pleasures and sorrows."

[Note: In every chapter of this book, I have felt the presence of God's love in the words and parables written. However, it is in writing this chapter about the Holy Spirit that I heard His voice. The night before writing this chapter, I struggled with how to write about the Holy Spirit and prayed for guidance. The next morning, I awoke to a man's voice speaking to me. The words in italics are those spoken to me that morning while the words that follow are those that came through my soul onto paper immediately after hearing His voice. Although I have changed many other chapters, this chapter remains as it was written that early morning.]

Chapter 10

Tears of Truth Lead to Joy

Many songs or books or movies always lead people to cry. Most of these do so with an immeasurable depth because they strike at the core of Truth, reverberating throughout the listener, the reader, or the viewer—reminding them of their own shortcomings or blessings. *These are Tears of Truth. They not only move souls, they change them.* Soon, when they listen to the same song, read the same passage, or watch the same scene, it does not move them as before. This is because *Tears of Truth are not designed to lead to more tears—they lead to peace and joy, which is eventually without tears.*

Just as happiness can only lead to a smile—tears found in the promise of God's love can only lead to joy. *While we know that the eyes are the windows of our soul, what is less known is that it is tears that cleanse them—not just our eyes, but also our souls.*

In joy, we understand what was once in darkness. Tears come forth because of the revelation of Truth—to see our own faults, or to see our many blessings taken for granted. These tears cleanse our souls.

And tears of Truth are not puppets to be replayed at will. Occasionally, we may relive our finding Truth in a tearful remembrance, but once in joy, it is love that surrounds us. *To the extent that we have forgotten the lessons of Truth—forgotten our own faults or taken for granted again our own blessings—tears of Truth will once again overcome us.* For these individuals, Truth will again shake them to the core. In Grace, and seeing Truth, we are reminded again of God's love.

Tears of Truth lead to joy. Tears not of Truth simply lead to more tears.

Chapter 11

Holy Matrimony (or Holy Orders)

Holy matrimony between a man and a woman is one of the seven Holy Sacraments of the Roman Catholic Church: 1) Baptism; 2) Reconciliation (known as "confession"); 3) The Holy Eucharist (known as "communion"); 4) Confirmation; 5) Holy Matrimony; 6) Holy Orders; and, 7) Anointing of the Sick.

The union of a husband and wife is holy because of what *it is* and what *it represents*. It is holy because *it is an open bond of mutual love, expressed in the offer of oneself and the acceptance of the other*. It is holy because *it is the heart of the family, the core to be united to bring forth new life*. It is *also* holy because *it is the deepest of bonds between people: the commitment of a man and a woman to each other in good times and in bad, in sickness and in health, until death do they part. And it is the blood that connects parents and children, brother and sister, aunts and uncles, grandparents and grandchildren. It is the rock upon which our society is built.*

Marriage is also holy because of what *it represents*. In this union, a man and a woman have offered themselves to the other in rejection of self-love, similar to what each of us must do to enter heaven. *By accepting the freely given love of the other, as God intended, they have overcome the knowledge of their own faults and misgivings and found themselves worthy of love*. It is the crossing of this gulf that brings a man and a woman on earth nearest to heaven. *In this way, marriage represents a sort of heaven on earth.*

For those who have accepted Holy Orders, they too are similarly "married" and joined on earth as in heaven. For a priest, it is through marriage to the Mother Church. For a nun, it is through marriage to our Lord Jesus Christ. *Even more so than Holy Matrimony, Holy Orders allow individuals to marry on earth and most closely mirror the actual union we hope to have with God in heaven.*

Chapter 12

Singlehood

During a mass I attended awhile back, the priest asked the congregation, "Are you married in heaven?" Of those present, most raised their hands to say, "Yes." He then pointed out that you are not married in heaven. During the sacrament of Holy Matrimony, he said that the priest asks both the bride and the groom, "Do you accept so-and-so until death do you part?" He went on to say that you are not a polygamist in heaven if you remarry after a spouse dies. In fact, it is because of this *primary union between God and the individual* that priests and nuns do not participate in the sacrament of holy matrimony. As they and we will be one with God in heaven, they have chosen to live their lives on earth as close to a heavenly existence as humanly possible—by joining in union with God here.

Singlehood *is* a holy profession. *Most are called and freely choose to marry between a man and a woman, but one should not be distressed if singlehood is thrust upon them, such as in not being able to find the right spouse, or having a spouse leave them out of self-love.* It is an opportunity to bring oneself closer to a heavenly existence and through prayer and free will, provides opportunities anew to find the right spouse, heal an ailing relationship, or to live a holy single life.

It is in this way that singlehood and one's relationship with God is of the greatest importance. Whether unmarried or joined in Holy Matrimony here on earth, one is not married in heaven. In communion with God, the angels and saints and others in heaven, *oneness with God and our Lord Jesus Christ through the Holy Spirit is only attainable in rejection of self-love and the giving of oneself to God.*

Chapter 13

Prayer

We communicate with God through prayer. And it is through prayer that we communicate to God our decisions. He does not need us to pray to Him to tell him what we need. He knows what we need before we ask.

He does not need us to tell Him what we are thinking. He already knows.

In almost every way, He does not need us to tell Him anything about our lives. He knows *everything* about us—to even knowing how many hairs we have on our head. But He chooses to let us decide the actions we will take.

We often do not know our direction, so we ask for help. *It is our decision to ask for help that communicates our decision that we love God—and it is through this loving request in prayer that we open the door to receiving God's love and mercy.* "Ask, and you will receive; seek, and you will find." (Luke 11:9)

Prayer should always be an integral part of the path to making up our minds. God does not need to travel the path—but we do. And He will travel patiently with us, if we are sincere. Frequently, He will reveal the answer just as we need it. This is not so much because He wishes us to wait but because it often takes us that long to see and accept His love completely.

Sometimes we need to pray to get our hearts to where they belong. *In other words, sometimes we have to pray to be able to pray.* Feeling wronged by God, we stop believing what we know is true. Like having a hole in one's heart, we may need to pray first to close the hole—which may take time.

Many years ago, I met a second woman who lost a brother to cancer and watched him die in a very painful way. This made her very upset and angry with God. Growing up, she always said her prayers at night, or as her grandmother taught her, she at least made the sign of the cross before bedtime as a sign of faith. But now she could not even make the sign of the cross, let alone pray.

With the help of a friend, she opened herself to the idea that God did exist. Over time, and in prayer to be able to pray, she was able to make the sign of the cross again before bedtime. And with this small act of faith, she was able to pray. But she had the humility to ask Him for help.

Prayers *are* answered, even those that are returned "no" or "not now." *Imagine the growing weight of trust you are building just by asking—asking every day.*

Chapter 14

Evil Thoughts

Anyone who has ever exercised free will on earth has had evil thoughts cross their minds. Everyone. Even Jesus, tempted by the devil in the desert to give up all that he believed in for earthly pleasure and power, experienced temptation and was confronted with its paradox of seemingly achieving all of what one seeks—in a quick and easy fashion.

But evil is still evil, and if you seek eternal life, it can never be found through evil. The paradox of the question put forth to us by the devil is "why trust God when evil can give you what you want today?" It is a paradox because eternal life *can* be found in a quick and easy fashion—today. It is before you to say "yes." The hard part is that we are not asked to say "yes" once, but *every day*. Fortunately, with every passing day that we say "yes," it is easier. There is always the risk that we will fail, but we become stronger with every day that we say "yes."

Sometimes, people feel guilty for even having evil thoughts cross their minds. *It's a mistake to agonize that they have been before you—even Christ was tempted by the devil.* Simply pray to choose not to act on them and avoid them in the future.

It is well known that everything good comes from God—"from whom all good things come." *What is less understood is that temptation to act on evil thoughts are also not your own.* As Jesus said, "Wicked designs come from the deep recesses of the heart . . . all these evils come from within . . ." (Mark 7:21-23) We also know God created Man with goodness, which is His love. *Temptation, the opportunity to embrace evil, is presented in circumstances outside you, and has as its proponent, the devil.* Just as opportunities to embrace and act out of goodness come from the Holy Spirit, temptation to act out evil comes from outside you and is advocated by the work of the devil. *Turn your back to temptation. It is when you give in to temptation that the evil in your heart can take root.* Protect yourself, your family, and others, and avoid the near occasion of sin.

Chapter 15

Temptation

When it comes to evil, we're often simplistic in our belief that we can withstand any temptation that might be presented to us. *We believe we can say "no" at any time. And yet, addictions that exist are very powerful, whether they are drugs, sex, pornography, materialism, or general self-indulgence.*

One illustration of the misunderstanding of the power of evil is the example of a man who thinks he can be a lineman on a football team but doesn't know his own size and strength or that of his competitor. There is a real risk that he will get seriously hurt.

Another example is a woman who says she can play tennis with anybody. And yet, if she were to play the No. 2 tennis player in the world, she would probably be crushed.

Evil may not be the No. 1 seed in life, but even as the No. 2 seed (and remember, Lucipher was God's greatest angel, or No. 2, until he decided to reject Him), the devil with his demons and addictions can be a formidable foe.

God allows temptation in the world as an opportunity for us to overcome sin. Have you ever noticed how some temptations overcome some people easily and others are not affected at all? This is because people have different thresholds of temptation and some people have learned how to avoid temptation in their hearts—even if they are exposed to temptation in their physical surroundings—even if they are more predisposed to sin.

Temptation offers an opportunity to become closer to God. In this way, we each have the opportunity to learn how to avoid temptation and increase our individual thresholds of temptation to become closer to God as God intended. And we can learn from others.

Pray to avoid temptation and pray to resist sin. As Jesus said, "The spirit is strong, but the flesh is weak." By learning to avoid our own thresholds of temptation, we become stronger in our resistance to sin.

Chapter 16

Proof of God

God can never be "proven" to exist as we define "proof" in science, with its measurable qualities and its ability to be replicated. At any given moment we may have proof of God's existence, but unlike science, we cannot see *everything*, the way God sees *everything*. God takes into account circumstances we cannot measure and cannot understand exactly, and thus, these individual moments cannot be replicated. Proof remains a gift to accept that which we cannot fully understand in a scientific way.

At the end of the movie, "The Song of Bernadette,"* actor Vincent Price, the town lawyer, ends the movie by saying, "to those who believe, no proof is necessary. To those who do not believe, no proof is great enough."

It exposes well the divide between believers and nonbelievers. *Believers see and hear—and believe. Nonbelievers see and hear—and ask to see and hear again.*

---

* *The Song of Bernadette,* Twentieth Century Fox Film Corporation, © 1943, Renewed © 1971.

Chapter 17

How Much Proof Is Enough?

How often do you need proof that God exists? Once a day? Once a week? How about once a month? *Or would you be satisfied to have unequivocal proof that God exists just once in your life?*

Most of us would say, *"Just once."* And yet, even after viewing the miracle of a birth of a child or the cure of illness, or another circumstance that we know is a miracle—we still look for more—as if we don't have any proof.

How foolish we are to always ask, "What have you done for me lately?" God's love is always present—it is just that we don't always see it.

Proof can come in the form of miracles or revelations. *In a way, we are students of the miracles and revelations that God sends to us.* Do you write them down? Already, I have forgotten two things that happened in the past two weeks that were almost certainly a result of divine intervention. It is so silly to forget.

And little miracles do occur. An interruption does not occur while completing a key task. Another time, everything that could conceivably go right does. Little miracles working peacefully and quickly—do you see them?

As for revelations, have you stopped for a moment to *know* that God is communicating with you? Are you listening? Do you bother to remember his revelations to you? *God wants us to see Him in our lives because He is always there.* And He desires for you to discover the Truth that He is real.

Chapter 18

Love is Like a Dove

Love is like a dove. If frightened, it will fly away. If you wish to provide it a home, you must feed it and nurture it. If you wish for it to grow, it must be shown love in order to respond with love. With time, it can be befriended or it can be lost. But its beauty is the same whether for a glimpse or a lifetime in its presence.

Love needs communication followed up by actions because, like a dove, it cannot always read minds—especially when our minds are not made up. And it is fragile, most notably when young and during every stage of growth. It assumes danger, and here it tends to overreact to protect itself. It can fly away from real danger or it can fly away from perceived danger—so even though we might end up wanting it to stay, it may fly away because we cannot make up our minds and communicate our kind intentions.

An example of this is the man who loved his wife and his work. In every day circumstances, his work always operated with appointments and rationalization. Meanwhile, the time he had with his wife were simply those that were leftover. They were without priority and done without the thoughtful deliberation he had done at work. Whether it was time, thoughtfulness, or energy, she only got what he had not used somewhere else. Soon she grew cold and no longer responded to the little things he would do for her. Going out to dinner, helping around the house, spending time with the children—doing whatever she would ask—they were now only drops of water on a dry cloth. These actions did not satisfy, and they did not give peace to him or to her.

Her love for him was like a dove. She always extended love and desired his love, but she needed to *trust* his love. If it was real, it couldn't be just an afterthought or what was left over. *She needed to know that he really loved her.*

He made an intentional decision to change his priorities. Through communication and quiet time together, first by arranging dates, and then by lifestyle, he tamed the beast of work and outside influence.

Now, love lives in their hearts and in their lives. And like a dove, whose trust is built over time, it returns love when it is shown love.

Chapter 19

Happy Are Those Who Fear the Lord

Ought we be a "God-loving" or a "God-fearing" people? The answer is not one or the other but both. *We love God because he has done great things for us.* He has provided us fruit from the earth and given us minds to help us help ourselves. *But we also "fear" Him in a way that is based in love.* He offered us eternal life and we chose death long ago. In his mercy, He established a way for us to be saved and to be reunited with Him in eternal life—but it is not a path that is wide and short.

When investing money in the marketplace, it is fundamental that if you want to maximize your chances for success you must diversify risk. This is simply saying that under a wide set of circumstances, you must hold your wealth in a manner so as not to be devastated by any one event. It is similar in our love of the Lord. *We must protect our love of God from a wide set of circumstances that can confront us in life, from devastating to tremendous success.* Some of these circumstances will result from the exercise of free will, that of ours or another, while other circumstances will be directly from God. Although we can say that "devastating" events make up only a small portion of immediate risk—it is real. Are you prepared to withstand them? There is also great risk when you experience success. Are you prepared for success as well?

Short-term risk is enough reason "to fear the Lord," but when one considers the long-term risk of something devastating happening, caused by us, caused by others, or directly by Him, it is even more reason to "fear the Lord." We cannot know exactly when God exacts just punishment on ourselves or others, just as we cannot know exactly why he would allow our own or others' free will or nature to harm us, but we do know that His love for us cannot be compromised. *Similarly, we must also be prepared for success. After years of struggling for success, it can happen quickly.*

Are you prepared to reject temptation, even when it is presented in the trappings of success?

Fear of God and love of God are not mutually exclusive but connected because of original sin and God's redeeming love for us—to forgive our sins—if we choose to love Him. Fear because we introduced pain and suffering in our lives years ago and thus must respect just punishment for our sins, including pain and suffering that can result from others' and our own free will. And love, which is what God meant for us from the beginning, is offered to us anew through the gift and example of His Son, Jesus Christ. We are wise to be a God-fearing *and* a God-loving people—by avoiding temptation and embracing His love.

Chapter 20

My Way Versus His Way

In 1998, my wife and I conceived a baby. He would be our third child and only son. Because of two previous miscarriages, she took hormone supplements to safeguard the pregnancy. The treatments made her sicker than she would be in a normal pregnancy, but also more aware than most of the growing baby in her womb.

During the sixth month, my wife knew something was not right. She asked me about her belly that now sagged. I noticed it, too, but I covered up my concern.

While going to the hospital and at the hospital, I prayed. I prayed in silence and with my wife. I begged God to spare our son and find life in his infant body. But it did not happen. The doctor told us our baby boy had died. The doctor would have to induce labor.

My way. It was my way that he should live. It was me who begged God to give life to our son.

Our way versus His way. After five agonizing days in the hospital and a series of unsuccessful attempts to induce labor, we could only feel sadness and pain.

Our way. On the fifth day, we finally gave up hope that labor could be induced. Our baby was inside, without life, and unable to be with us.

And then—we opened our way to His way. We embraced God's will without condition. If He wanted us to have the baby in the hospital—we would accept it. If He wanted us to go home and wait—we would accept that as well.

As our will was broken to accept His, our son, Philip James Gauthier, was delivered. Emitted still in the sac, he was an angel. In us, around us, and with us, he shone love on us without a sound. *Warmth and sweetness, peace and innocence, we could feel only joy in seeing his face for the first time.*

I did not plan to take his picture. If he were alive in my wife's womb, we would wait many more weeks for his birth. If he were dead, I could not imagine wanting a picture. But then he arrived and was in our arms. Moments later, I went down to the gift shop to buy a camera to remember his angel face. The clerk, who I'm sure had seen many newborn fathers, recognized my disheveled look with the purchase of a camera.

She asked, "A boy or a girl?" I could only respond with tears in my eyes, "A boy, but he did not live."

Back in the delivery room, taking pictures of joy and holding our new baby boy, we cherished the three hours we had with him. No further proof was needed to know that our God was real, even if His will took us toe-to-toe with our own.

During these three hours, our parish priest visited us and held him as well. He had never held a dead infant in his arms, but we wanted to share with him pure love. *Knowing his soul was already where we wanted to be, he told us that little Philip was now our advocate—to help us join Him in heaven.*

We expected our son's birth to be a source of joy and hope—we just didn't know that it would be His way, and not ours.

Chapter 21

Pain and Suffering

We are often faced with the reality that pain and suffering exist despite our efforts to eliminate it, or at least mitigate it.

Pain and suffering is not separate from joy; in fact, pain and suffering is part of how joy is gained. Persons full of joy are sometimes consumed by pain and suffering. For example, joy in giving is often associated with pain, such as the joy of working or sacrificing to make another person's life easier.

On rare occasions, complete joy and pain and suffering are concurrent, such as at the death of St. Joan of Arc, who joyfully martyred to save her country. But for most, pain and suffering are simply integral to joy because they precede it. In a sense, without suffering, there would be no joy. Without working hard, you cannot be successful. Without discipline, you cannot achieve your goals.

By knowing the depths of pain, we can appreciate joy. By feeling pain and suffering, we can achieve greater understanding of love. For an athlete in training, it's "no pain, no gain." It is similar in spiritual life.

Pope John Paul II said, "Divine revelation helps us understand that suffering is not desired by God, but has entered the world because of sin. God allows suffering for the very salvation of man, drawing good out of evil."*

On earth, we have the fullness of knowledge of *how* life works, but not the knowledge of *why*. When we accept the mystery of pain and suffering and have complete faith, we will enable ourselves to find peace and joy and everlasting life. *We cannot fully understand why, but we can understand how.*

---

*   Weekly Wednesday address as reported in *The Catholic News and Herald.*

Chapter 22

More on Pain and Suffering

God's will required His Son to die on the cross for us. *What do you think "His will" will require of you?*

During the course of life, from birth to death, pain will occasionally absorb you. Do you hold it like a treasure or do you despise it? Even after exercising our free will to reduce pain, it still surrounds us. Do you see the purpose of pain? Do you see its cleansing purpose—it's glory? Washing and scrubbing, scraping and molding, it draws us closer to Him.

In good times, it is easy to confuse the causes of joy amidst all the noise. *But in bad times, such as in pain and suffering, we listen more attentively and thus God speaks more clearly, showing us the way to His eternal love.*

And God will not send you more than you can handle. Mother Teresa said this frequently in her life. In one of my favorite quotes she underscores not only her ability to accept God's difficult challenges, but how to accept them with joy and even with humor. She said to laughter at the National Prayer Breakfast in 1994, "I wish God didn't trust me so much." God will never send you more than you can handle, but like Mother Teresa, you will be amazed at how much you can.

For those who might confuse pain and suffering as introduced by man's original sin with pain and suffering imposed by man's free will, we are not to purposefully inflict physical or emotional pain on ourselves or others. *Pain and suffering occur despite our efforts to mitigate them. When we willfully cause pain and suffering to others or ourselves, it is a sin because it is outside of God's will and, like all sin, separates the sinner from God.* For those who have lost a friend or relative to suicide, take comfort in knowing that only God knows completely the circumstances. God lovingly holds in His arms His own.

Chapter 23

Isn't It Selfish to Pursue Joy?

While traveling, a young person once asked me, "Isn't it selfish to pursue joy? to pursue the joy of heaven?" I responded to her with a question: "If someone wanted to give you a gift and would receive great joy if you were to accept it, is it selfish for you to receive it?"

It is not "selfishness" as we know it to accept God's love—even though his love is the greatest gift we can ever receive—*because it gives God great joy when we accept it.*

Does a mother consider her baby "selfish" for seeking to be fed? Of course not. She so desires to feed her baby that it is impossible for the baby to be selfish. It gives her great pleasure to feed her baby—even if the baby's actions result in its own comfort and joy. *Both the giver and receiver experience the joy of love because it is absent of self-love.* In fact, the pursuit of God's everlasting joy requires suffering in giving and suffering in receiving, such as in living, even though both will achieve complete joy.

I have often thought, how much time and attention should a man give to his wife, his mother, and his mother-in-law? As Mother Teresa taught us, "give until it hurts." He must give of himself in many acts of kindness. And he must give of himself out of pleasure—not out of just sacrifice. In joy, he must give until it hurts. *When he does, he will find he is doing God's will.* Heartfelt love is necessary. In joy, we must give until it hurts. *When we do this, we will have given to a point where we break our own will to do God's.*

In the end, the question is not really about whether you care about your spouse, your parent, or your in-law—even though you will if you accept God's love. *The question is whether you care about yourself—and love God.* You will show that you love God when you acknowledge that he has done great things for you and know in your heart that you are worthy of love—worthy of the greatest love of all—God's.

While it may seem selfish to do these things when we know it will lead to joy—to give to others until it hurts and, thus, accept God's love—it is the path to saving your own soul. And it would please God.

Chapter 24

Sin and Reconciliation with God

The most difficult aspect of sin for the one who has sinned is seeking forgiveness. But it is not the seeking of forgiveness from others that is the most difficult, even though necessary. *When feeling truly sorry, the most difficult actions for a sinner are to ask for forgiveness from God and to forgive yourself. You cannot truly receive God's forgiveness without forgiving yourself.* How often do we ask others to forgive us when we are not ready to forgive ourselves? We continue to carry forward guilt, an unhealthy form of guilt, ignoring our own request and God's subsequent forgiveness. Or possibly, how many times have we asked for forgiveness when in our hearts we don't really believe we have sinned? *It is impossible to receive forgiveness when we are not really sorry—and thus not ready to receive it.*

Forgiving oneself is always in full view of God—and perhaps that is why it is so difficult. It is even more difficult when you ask for forgiveness from God through someone else—someone in the flesh. Even before Jesus' first prophesy of his coming death and resurrection, He told Simon Peter, "You are 'Rock,' and on this rock I will build my church." (John 16:18) Jesus also told him, "Whatever you declare bound on earth shall be bound in heaven; whatever you declare loosed on earth shall be loosed in heaven." (John 16:19)

This helps explain how the church requires reconciliation before a priest. Life-changing decisions are first made from within, but are then made stronger when spoken to another. It is too easy to have a private conversation with God and ask for forgiveness when it is absent of human interaction. Facing your sins in person requires the deepest commitment of regret and promise to improve. *And asking forgiveness from one of God's chosen priests is critically important.* Jesus granted St. Peter the power to absolve or not to absolve our sins—the same authority St. Peter and his successors have made available to you through your local priest.

When Jesus visited the apostles after his resurrection, he breathed the Holy Spirit on them and told them "whatever you declare bound on earth shall be bound in heaven; whatever you declare loosed on earth shall be loosed in heaven." Even though He granted this authority to St. Peter, who was "rock," He revealed that He wanted this ministered by many—by those who were the chosen "fishers of men."

One can only imagine the strength of absolution as Jesus directed. It is when forgiveness is sought and then granted, as Jesus taught us, that it is most successfully life changing.

When we seek forgiveness, we are seeking forgiveness from God. It is a belief that God can forgive sins. It is real. When He forgives you, do you really accept it? Do you forgive yourself?

Chapter 25

Happiness and Money

Every man seeks financial security for his family. He seeks to give them all they need, a house, food, and modern comforts. He may view money as a cure and a means to thwart pain that his family might suffer, but in the end, he risks losing the love of his wife and his children.

This happened to a man I know. Viewing money as an end, those around him grew selfish and he felt used. Soon, the family longed for the love they had always had but did not nourish. *Although they shared wealth, they did not share love. Money was not an end, and even as a means, not the most important thing.* In the end, they realized what many had learned before—that money can never be the source of happiness.

Is money the most important thing to you? What is *your* bottom line?

In our lives, it is easy to hoard money, or to spend it only on ourselves. *Do you give to others? Do you even know that others need help? In church, do you give from the first fruits, or just the surplus?*

Chapter 26

Listening and Talking

Do you have the patience to listen?

If you are the one talking, do you have the courage to be thoughtful?

Even though we must be grounded in Truth to keep from being entrapped or snared by sin, many people are not prepared for life's challenges and its fragility. We must prepare ourselves. We must learn.

In a memorable homily, my pastor said, *"Truth is the greatest gift we can give to each other. It can be found in and learned from any man or woman."**

Are we listening for Truth? And when we hear of and learn about Truth, do we use it to prepare us for life?

We must talk to and, more importantly, listen to others. We are only one among many.

---

*   Rev. Msgr. John J. McSweeney

Chapter 27

If You Put a Pot of Water on the Stove
And Turn It on "High," It Will Boil

It is well documented the differences between men and women and how they are sexually aroused. Men are usually aroused easily by visual stimuli while women take a combination of the senses—very distinct from men.

Knowing this, *"Why do we constantly bombard ourselves with temptation?"* If you put a pot of water on the stove and turn it on high—it will boil. Similarly, high exposure to temptation will lead to arousal. It will happen.

Sexual arousal between a man and a woman is proper, desired, and holy in the union between a husband and a wife. Why would we want to cheapen it by pornography or incessant public images that can only be described as seeking arousal outside of a Holy union? *Abstinence from sex on occasion, especially through natural family planning, and faithfulness when apart, helps to build a foundation of love. It is not the pleasure of the moment, but the fullness of love—and its overwhelming permanent ecstasy—which we should seek.* It is sexier, more fulfilling, and desired in God's eyes.

Chapter 28

Tolerance and Love

Today, more than ever in recent history, sexual activity in its many forms outside of a union of a man and a woman has become acceptable in our culture. Although more commonplace, this does not mean it is God's will.

Jesus gave us insight into how to view others' sins when asked by the elders, 'What should we do with the sinner who has committed adultery?' Jesus, said, "Let the person without sin cast the first stone." More specifically, in the case of homosexuality, as stated in the Catechism of the Catholic Church, "They must be accepted with respect, compassion, and sensitivity. Every sign of unjust discrimination in their regard should be avoided."*

The path to God's will is one that includes sacrifice and suffering, and requires one to empty oneself of self-pride. The blind pursuit of temporal pleasure without a moral compass will inevitably stray from God's will.

Through love, embracing God's gifts to us—whether they are burdensome or light (and we know they are light and easy when we have faith)—we can persevere and enjoy our circumstances even if God may compel some to sacrifice and suffer more than others.

Many years ago, I knew a student confused by the many sexual options presented to him by popular culture. He thought, "Is homosexuality wrong? Isn't this just another form of creative expression?" He was pressured by prejudiced parents, peers, and family members. "Weren't they closed in their minds and incapable of seeing Truth?" And yet, he knew Truth was blind. What was the Truth?

---

* Catechism of the Catholic Church, ©1994.

Over the course of a lifetime, he would find that discovering *how life works* would be at times hazy, winding, or hidden. All will travel it and all deserve the opportunity to find it. *But he would also learn that tolerance and love should be our response to others who are lost—embracing the goodness in deeds, words, and the souls of all people, whoever they are, including sinners—even as we as a society must establish laws that set the boundaries of civil behavior.*

Eventually, he would discover homosexuality was wrong because it was not God's will and it was not as God intended. *In the end, he would recognize that man's creativity and the desire to explore creativity are gifts that can lead men and women to stray from God's will and into homosexuality and onto other paths away from God.* And yet, God's promise of love is there regardless of whether or not our creative expression is in harmony with God's will. *The irony is that we must use our creative expression to see Him working in our lives—and some of our greatest opportunities to see Him are lost because of the misdirected use of creative expression.* Even though we are allowed to be lost, He is waiting for us to see how He works in our lives—waiting for us to choose to embrace His love for us—to love Him.

In a spiritual sense, even Jesus "loved" his friends. It is just that in a physical sense love is reserved for the holiest of unions—between a man and a woman. God has always set rules, and we have always been tempted to violate them, but they are in place for a reason—to bring us closer to Him and to help us live our lives more fully. Over time, He promises that we will find His perfect love for us.

The student decided to live his life in tolerance, but not in indifference. To be indifferent to sin, especially to the young and the naïve who risk falling into the snare of sin, would be to implicitly endorse it. No, he would live his life with patience, accepting others with respect, compassion, and sensitivity who are at a different point on the path of life, but also open to the return of the sinner. Ready to help others resist choosing a path away from God's will.

Chapter 29

Creativity

God gave us creativity and wants us to be creative to find His will. In fact, creativity—the ability to see what others do not—and living God's will, are connected. God's will requires creativity in order to find and live His will.

Have you ever noticed that the greatest acts of "creativity" are called "discoveries?" This is not to disrespect the thoughtfulness, courage, and tenacity of the people who worked long hours, struggled to put together disparate parts, and found remarkable solutions to difficult problems. It is a realization that these acts are really only unveiling what was true all along—only hidden.

In combination, new "discoveries" along with previous "discoveries" lead to new inventions, new explorations, and even new art forms. These inventions and creative expressions could have existed much sooner if man had known these principles and properties before, but they are a result of the creative process.

Creativity in a more common form, far short of these great discoveries, is simply an individual's discovery of his or her own point on the path to Truth. When we are pushed aside, from circumstances or by others' actions, we find a new position on the path to Truth. And yet, despite being something we all must do, *finding our own point on the path to Truth is the point from which our salvation is made easier or more difficult.*

At work or at play, or through the various forms of art—these are all creative expressions that can help us on our path to Truth, to make our salvation easier—if we direct our creative energies to be in harmony with God's will.

How will you know if you are using your creative expression in harmony with God's will? You will be at peace and in joy in God's love. This is the same for those around you—and we impact each other. You cannot fully understand it; but you will know it.

Chapter 30

Sin

Man introduced sin into the world through his own free will thousands of years ago. Then and now, God does not want us to sin—he wants us to live without sin. In fact when we sin, we separate ourselves from God.

When we are overcome by temptation and sin against God, the first thing we can do to please God is to stop such sin—just as Jesus told the prostitute to go and sin no more. Next, we can work to avoid temptation. Sometimes temptations are so strong we will succumb despite our initial attempts to resist—the flesh is weak, the spirit is strong—but our best defense is always to avoid temptation. Avoiding sin may mean turning off or not surfing your television, avoiding sinful Web sites, or not opening sinful attachments and e-mail (you can guess which ones they are), avoiding sinful environments, and even sinful people—all of these become our best defense.

There is no shame in being tempted, especially after you have tried to minimize your risk, because temptation comes from outside you. It is your response that counts.

Consider the person who struggled with what to give up for Lent. He knew that it ought to be something of a sacrifice, but he also knew that it should not be something frivolous. To him, it would be simply superficial to give up ice cream or cake or candy or some other item—especially if he did not embrace the message of Lent to cleanse his heart throughout his life. For example, what good would it do to give up dessert at lunch if he did not treat his colleagues with love after lunch?

He decided to give up sin.

As you might guess, he did not accomplish his objective, but his goal and his efforts were right. *At little moments of decision where he could choose gluttony or sacrifice, he chose sacrifice. At little moments when his heart could choose sin, he chose holiness.* He improved his love for God and his family. *Eventually, by asking, he knew he would receive.*

Upon leaving church after receiving ashes on Ash Wednesday, he was immediately confronted with his first temptation. Should he wipe off his ashes and hide his faith, or leave the ashes on his forehead for all to see? Knowing that he would take pleasure in wiping them off—he left them on—his own little cross to carry for the day.

He also knew he could not be indifferent to sin and evil. *Others who are still deciding their own fate or destiny depend on his and others' guidance and example.* While we must be tolerant to always leave open the door for others' return from sin, we cannot pretend the consequences of the choices are the same without sinning ourselves.

Chapter 31

Children of God

Are you living your life as a Child of God? *Or do you carry burdens that only an adult would have?* Jesus wants us to live our lives as Children of God.

Have you ever heard the innocence of a child asking for something? Asking, "Can I go with you?" *This is how God wants us to ask to enter heaven.*

In everyday life, children constantly give us examples on how to live. Years ago, my youngest daughter was confronted with the conflicting messages about death that we all must deal with. Even though a family friend would soon die, she was told that she should be happy because he would soon be with baby Jesus. She was also told that it would be sad because he would no longer be with us. She said, *"I understand. It is happy and sad."*

Jesus said, "Let the children come to me; for the kingdom of heaven belongs to those such as these."

It is with innocence and purity that God wants us to live our lives— *to embrace goodness with the trust and acceptance of a child's understanding.*

Chapter 32

The Misunderstanding of "Women Be Submissive to Your Husbands"

One of the greatest misunderstandings of the Bible is the phrase, "Women be submissive to your husbands." It conjures up images for both men and women of husbands dominating their wives. This interpretation is wrong and firmly clarified in our parish congregation by a young, newly-ordained priest. Every sin, he explained, is a result of man not trusting that what hasbeen promised will be given to him.

He went on to say that man dominates because of the fear that what has been promised will not be given. And yet, being one with God is not something to be taken. If you want to be one with God's will, the mission is to "empty yourself."

Have you ever heard the phrase, 'So-and-so is full of himself?' Or, 'so-and-so is full of herself?' *To empty oneself, one must first be empty of self-pride.*

In Ephesians, Ch. 5, it states: 'Wives be submissive to your husbands, as to God.' For some women, he said, this is read to be even more extreme than submissive—that is, to be submissive to their husbands as if he is God. But what this really says is that *man is called to give his life to his wife as God has done for us.* A woman is called to accept man's willingness to give his life and empty herself as all of us are called to empty ourselves before God.

Quite beautiful, I think—and opposite of the popular interpretation of this passage. A man gives himself to his wife and a wife accepts her husband's giving of himself as she accepts God's giving of his life. And they both empty themselves for the other.

For men, the priest concluded his homily by asking 'do you dominate your bride or do you give yourself away as Christ? Or have you forsaken your mission, to give yourself away?'

For women, he similarly asked them 'do you accept the gift of your husband giving himself to you? Or have you forsaken your mission to give yourself away, such as through nagging or belittling?'

"Women be submissive to your husbands. Husbands, love your wives."

To live in Truth, men and women must empty themselves for the other.

Chapter 33

Where There Is No Faith,
There Are No Miracles

I'll use a parable here. There was a couple that over many years grew set in their individual ways. At first, they loved each other, even though they each had their own faults. Then, over time, the love they showed each other stopped showing up in little ways. The miracle of love, *which allows each of us to see beyond our own faults and accept that someone loves us*, began to erode away like a riverbank of sand.

They were now on the brink of divorce. She called her family to prepare them for what might happen. Lovingly, they listened and talked about the situation and worked with both of them to understand the other. And they prayed.

It would take a miracle. But with prayer, anything is possible.

Did you know that the first thing you should pray for when praying for someone is that they have faith? Faith is a gift, but each must accept it every day. The mystery of the gift itself is that you must empty yourself of everything that is not God's will in order to be filled with His. This includes misplaced pride, insistence on the outcome being 'your way,' or indulgence in earthly pleasures. And it is when you are "empty" that you will be "full." *Where is your faith in asking for the miracle? Are you ready to accept His will?*

Like the couple you might be praying for, or for that matter, a sick parent, an injured child, or for someone who is out of work, do you pray that they have faith? That they will be able to empty themselves and accept God's will?

Miracles can be as simple as a change of heart, a break in a fever or reduction of swelling, or an opportunity given. Do you see them? *God frequently requires action on our part to fulfill them—prayer and action. And He always requires that we accept His will.*

Miracles happen, they happen every day.

Jim and Phyllis Gauthier and Family, circa 1976

Gauthier Family Property – and the 'Big Top' fruit stand

Gauthier Family, circa 2016*

Surviving Gauthier siblings*

*Photos by Tonya Broad Wildfong.

Chapter 34

The Most Realistic People

There have been many studies showing a correlation between a person's inclination to be steadfastly realistic and prone to depression. In an earthly sense, this is not surprising. Pervasive problems such as racism, poverty, and discrimination, have shown their persistence despite years of efforts to address them.

But where is their faith? *Faith is our foundation which leads to hope and love*. With faith, we can overcome any obstacle and correct any wrong.

Realism based in an earthly sense will surely lead to depression—we can never fully trust in man. Realism based in faith will lead to hope and love—which is joy.

Chapter 35

Women Are In Touch

Women tend to be more affected by stress than men. This should not be surprising, as *women are generally in touch with everything and everyone around them—all the time.*

Is it genetic? Perhaps. Is it learned? Perhaps. But in one sense, *being intensely involved in your surroundings will certainly lead to stress.*

What is the solution? *Men can become more involved in their surroundings to relieve women of this burden, but women can also become more focused on the things that are most important and not simply everything.*

Chapter 36

The Most Misunderstood; Least Intuitively Known; And Most Gracious Advocate

Can you think of anyone whom you have fully loved who has not also loved your parents? *Just as we must honor our own parents to embrace God's love, we must also honor the parents of others.*

Do you remember when the rest of the world did not believe in you, but your parents did? Or, for those whose parents did not believe in them, do you remember when someone reminded you that your parents were lovable? Possibly even someone who showed you that your parents were lovable even after you had forgotten?

It is in these ways that we are called to love our parents, the parents of others, *and the parents of Jesus.*

In the Virgin Mary, we are given the purest example of how to live one's life in harmony with God's will. Conceived without sin, the only woman since Eve to be born so, she chose to use her free will to fulfill God's promise. In Joseph, a foster parent, we learn that man, even born in sin, can live a clean life, honoring God, setting an example for his child, and keeping in place his pride that could threaten all that is around him.

'How many of you think we worship Mary?' was a question put forth to my congregation. Two-thirds of the hands went up to say, "Yes." Then they were asked 'how many of you think Catholics do not worship Mary?' Realizing that they may have gotten the answer wrong, two-thirds of the hands went up again.

This is so telling because if Catholics do not know that they do not worship Mary, how can non-Catholics know? Catholics do not worship Mary. They pray to Mary for her intercession on their behalf to herSon—God the Father, God the Son, and God the Holy Spirit.

The only tool for obtaining the intercession of Mary is through prayer. No one worthy of her intercession has ever been refused. And requesting her assistance in asking for one of God's miracles is like asking for help through God's closest advisor. It works. And one of the best ways to ask for Mary's help is through the Holy Rosary. It is a source of infinite strength and represents an opportunity to affect the future through the act of prayer and free will. (And remember, even the act of prayer begins as an expression of free will.)

The Rosary begins with the Apostle's Creed, as we too are apostles of our Lord Jesus Christ. It then follows a repetition of our Lord's prayer and Hail Marys to follow every major event in the history of our salvation, our Lord Jesus Christ's announced coming, life, death, and resurrection separated into four sets of mysteries: Joyful, Luminous, Sorrowful, and Glorious.

Retracing Jesus' life, the joyful mysteries begin by remembering the Annunciation, when the Angel Gabriel delivers a message to the Virgin Mary that God would like her to bear a son to be called Jesus. Unlike Eve, Mary accepts God's will, and thus, our salvation begins to be made possible.

The remaining Joyful mysteries retrace the formative stages of our salvation: the Visitation, expressing the joy of knowing Jesus is coming; the Nativity, the birth of our Lord; the Presentation, introducing Jesus to the faithful; and the Finding in the Temple, when Mary and Joseph realize that Jesus' mission is to use his free will to be near his father. With this foundation, born and raised by the Virgin Mary and Joseph and presented to the faithful, He would teach us.

The Luminous mysteries represent the major points of Jesus' adult ministry prior to his passion and resurrection: the Baptism of Jesus by John the Baptist, when God announces that this is his beloved Son with whom He is well pleased; The Miracle at the Wedding at Cana, when Jesus performs his first miracle at the request of his mother; The Announcement of the Kingdom of Heaven and the call to conversion, when Jesus urges us to prepare for eternal life; the Transfiguration of Jesus with Moses and Elijah, when God announces to his disciples that this is His beloved Son and urges us to listen to Him; and the Institution of the Holy Eucharist, *Jesus' eternal ministry*, where His body and blood—eternal life and the forgiveness of sins—are present and available to us today.

The Sorrowful mysteries retrace Jesus' bending of his own free will to do his father's: The Agony in the Garden, Jesus' realization that our salvation requires him to suffer greatly; the Scourging at the Pillar, Jesus' suffering at the hands of his captors; the Crowning with Thorns, Jesus' humiliation borne by our mocking him; the Carrying of the Cross, Jesus' burden and pain to carry our sins; and the Crucifixion, the death of our Lord Jesus Christ to free us from our sins.

The Glorious mysteries begin with the Resurrection of Jesus, in fulfillment of the Scriptures. The second Glorious mystery, the Ascension, represents Jesus' leaving us in a humanly sense. The third Glorious mystery, the Descent of the Holy Spirit, represents Jesus' being present among us today in a new form.

The final two mysteries of the glorious mysteries, the Assumption of the Virgin Mary into heaven, and her Coronation as Queen of Heaven, are the most difficult to grasp but offer the sweetest comfort. The Assumption represents the completion of the Virgin Mary's life on Earth—born without sin, and having lived her life in purity, she is received in heaven body and soul—just as God had promised Eve. *Through her assumption, she is our hope that we, too, can choose to live our lives in harmony with God's will.* The Coronation of the Virgin Mary as Queen of Heaven announces that Mary has gained a special place in the heart of God the Father, God the Son, and God the Holy Spirit as a result of her life on earth. Through her coronation, this part of history unfolds as God intended, but it is only complete as a result of the use of her free will. God's will and the will of the Virgin Mary have been in harmony on earth, and now she is rewarded as Queen of Heaven. Through the use of her maternal free will, she has become the Mother of Mercy and is now our most gracious advocate.

Mary, full of grace and blessed among women, remained a virgin even as she conceived Jesus, the blessed fruit of her womb, through the Holy Spirit. And she lived a life of purity, bending her will to God's. Unlike Eve who was also born without sin, the Virgin Mary chose to live a life of purity. Her path was not without pain; she had to watch her only child die on the cross. But she also lived her life guiding her Son. She beseeched Him to perform his first miracle at the wedding at Cana years ago, turning water into wine, even though Jesus at first resisted. Similarly, she is available to us today as "Mary, Help of Christians."

God's glory is well defined: He is all-powerful. But man's course to him through history is defined by our own acts of free will and God's intervention as a result of prayer.

The Virgin Mary, the most misunderstood even by many who should know her better, is also the least intuitive because she is not the source of God's authority. And yet, *because of her love for her Son and His special love for His mother*, she offers comfort to all who have recourse to her—the love that can only be had when you honor Him by seeking the aid of His mother. Her role and His love for her are that great.

Chapter 37

The Brother of the Prodigal Son

Almost everyone is familiar with the story of the 'prodigal son,' especially the relationship between the father and the son. However, there is another figure in this story that deserves mention. The prodigal son had a brother who claimed to despise sin. We can surmise that throughout his life he condemned those who sinned, especially those who brought shame to their families. But like his brother—the prodigal son—he too, fell prey to sin.

By our own free will, we are able to stray from God's will. To the varying degree that we sin, we have that much further to come back. And yet, just as the prodigal son returned to a loving father—a righteous man who did not condone sin, but prayed for his son's return—this man, the brother of the prodigal son resented the celebration of his brother's return.

Instead, he kept a "holier than thou" attitude that is not based in the Holy Spirit. He observed the same circumstances as his father, and acknowledged that what his brother had done was wrong—but he only thought of himself when he asked his father why he had never offered him a party as grand as the one he offered his long lost brother. *All he offered was judgment.*

How do you direct your energies to those who are lost? Are you like the brother of the prodigal son—only thinking of yourself and offering judgment? Or the father, filled with forgiveness and love?

Chapter 38

More On the Brother of the Prodigal Son

A person might ponder, "I know that I should be more like the father of the prodigal son, but can't I revel in the prodigal son's agony for just a little while? Even for just a few moments?" The prodigal son had caused so much pain that certainly God would understand.

God always knows and understands the impact of our actions and inactions. The question is whether *we* know and understand. "Does reveling in another's shortcomings bring us closer to or put us farther away from God? And is not the humiliation of the prodigal son, the humiliation that will bring him closer to God, more stark when it exists without more sin around it?

Getting closer to God is our goal. God offers grace to the prodigal son, the father, and the brother every day. *Why would any of us refuse His love for even a little while?*

Every day, especially on days when we might sin by reveling in another's sin, we should pray and use our own free will to be closer to God. It was in the best interests of the prodigal son's brother; it is in the best interest of ourselves; and most importantly, it is how God wants us to live—by serving others.

Chapter 39

God and the Media

Have you ever noticed that songs or movies that can withstand the test of time to become "classics" are often interwoven with God's Truth? Or at least the honest pursuit of it? It is Truth that satisfies; and it is only in peace that we can find God's Truth.

Many songs contain references to God or religious phrases found in the Bible. This is probably because the search for Truth is eternal on earth—whether the truth of love or the dangers of evil.

And God is love. Thus, songs, movies or books about the pursuit, gain, or loss of love are always popular and in fashion. The act of physical love, pure and beautiful in marriage, can easily be confused with love that is not pure or right—just as the flesh can experience pleasure outside of God's will. But we are still drawn to Truth like a magnet is to steel. We can count numerous songs and lyrics referencing love, angels, and heaven—and our longing to be closer to Him, to know Truth. Unfortunately, many of these same songs bear false witness to love, angels, and heaven.

In the 1980s, for the first time, surveys showed that more Americans went to the movies every week than attended church services. This led one prominent movie director to say that movies had replaced the church in providing societal norms. On the one hand, it is encouraging that a leader in the movie industry would recognize the importance of its content in influencing Americans—from children to adolescents to adults. On the other hand, it is discouraging—judging by the content of the vast number of movies produced—that so few in the industry truly understand *how life works,* or are unable or unwilling to communicate it. As a result, it is very difficult for good to come from much of this work.

Meanwhile movies, songs, and books of Truth resonate. They are sought out for their thirst quenching qualities—but they are also difficult to produce. This is because Truth lives in, comes from, and through peace.

The difficulty with the mediums of computers, television, radio, and the movies is that they often run counter to what is needed first to get closer to God—peace. *It is not that Truth is impossible to communicate through these mediums; it is just inherently more difficult because of the mediums themselves.* These mediums have to overcome the obstacle of a lack of peace in order to present Truth.

And music most nearly matches the emotion of the soul. Or as my wife says, 'music most beautifully evokes the emotion of the soul.' This is perhaps how it has become a critical element of virtually every medium, for every purpose.

Songs with references to heaven and love resonate Truth—and our minds catch these phrases. But too often, these references are false. Examples of these are songs that essentially say that 'truth' is whatever we want it to be. This is nonsense. *What is true is Truth, regardless of what we may believe right now, and hopefully some day we will get it right.*

Fortunately, most movies and television shows of the largest appeal are found in Truth—or at least by their honest pursuit of Truth—so there is hope.

Chapter 40

Peace Is Ours To Choose

"'Peace' is my farewell to you, my peace is my gift to you."
(John 15:27)

These words Jesus gave to us at the last supper over 2000 years ago. As Truth, it remains true yesterday, today and always. *Whether as individuals, families, communities, or countries, peace has already been given to us. But will we choose peace?*

Have you ever noticed that when you are at peace it spreads to those around you—such as the rest of your family? Or when someone else is not at peace, it spreads to you? It is like this at all levels, whether individuals, families, communities, or nations.

Peace is a house built upon a foundation, and that foundation is the individual (or better described, that individual's relationship with God). With peace from within you, first in your heart, and then in your marriage, the family finds peace. When families are at peace, communities are at peace. When communities are at peace, nations are at peace. And this is when we will have international peace.

Have you ever noticed that the solution to a problem often comes to you when you're doing something unrelated, doing something else at peace? St. Thérèse noticed this more than one hundred years ago. *It is in this way that the mysteries of life are revealed to us.* Peace is available to anyone who seeks it. We, too, must simply find peace in our hearts and listen.

Does peace come at a cost? If denying ourselves little things that our wills desire represents a "cost," then yes, throughout the levels of peace, there is a cost. At no level, from the foundation of the individual, to spouses in marriage, to families in the community, to communities in a nation, or between countries, can peace be found without a level of such "cost."

And the greatest cost is to give one's life for his friends, as Jesus did for us.

Are we willing to offer the little costs, and even the greatest cost, for peace?

Peace is ours to choose.

Chapter 41

But For the Grace of God

"But for the grace of God." It is a common thought among grateful people. And it is true. But it is not complete. *It omits a necessary part—the part of man's free will to accept God's love.*

This decision, to water the seed that God has planted in all of us, is entirely our own. It is what God is always waiting for, *but it is also what makes our love for Him real.*

His love is always available for us to see and accept, but only if we choose to open our eyes and embrace it. And when we accept His love we will see even more the graces of God in our lives.

Chapter 42

Love Versus Evil

Many embrace the Golden Rule as a way of life. But even among those who profess the "golden rule," not everyone believes in God, and many remain agnostic in their faith—especially given all of the violence and sinfulness in the world. And yet, each man and woman is given opportunities by God to do good or evil. Good helps others; evil hurts others. And as heart wrenching as it may seem that evil could be done to you or me or those we love, it can happen.

However, we can intervene through prayer. Prayer introduces the opportunity for God's will to be done, or after evil has been chosen, a new opportunity for God's will to be done.

Sometimes, we forget the things we pray for and when God finally answers 'yes,' we may have forgotten what we prayed for—or even changed our minds. This happens especially when we pray for something and also ask that it *only* be granted if it is what is *best* for us. How surprised we are when God answers 'yes' to our most important request!

God's answers to our prayers are rooted in his ever-present love for us. *And God grants us love, even when our requests are selfish or self-serving.* It may just take time for us to see His love.

And evil can happen as a result of our own or others' free will. It is not what God desires, but evil can happen.

For those who have chosen to use your free will to embrace goodness and reject evil—thank you!

Chapter 43

One God

How can there be so many religions? Is there really only one true God?

There is much less division among the faiths than we may have been led to believe. For example, the Ten Commandments exist in the Jewish, Christian, and Islamic faiths. Another example is that both Christian and Islamic faiths believe that Jesus was born of a virgin—the Virgin Mary.

Throughout history, proof has been provided of the one God—sometimes even to clarify previously unconfirmed facts—such as the 19th-century apparitions that revealed the Virgin Mary was born without sin—the Immaculate Conception.

Everyone who believes in God, if they are on a sincere path to find Truth, will find the one true God. An example of this is the belief by many religions who embrace in some form or another "The Golden Rule: To do unto others as you would have done unto you." This is found in Buddhism (Udana—Varga 5:18); Confucianism (Analects 15:23); Hinduism (Mahabharata 5:1517); Judaism (Talmud, Shabbat 3id); Islam (Sunnah); and Christianity (Matthew 7:12).

How long we travel and how lost we become depends on them and us. *Truth is revealed to all—so we may learn from each other—but divine truth remains the same, no matter who we are and where we travel.*

"Gentile or Jew, servant or free, woman or man, no more." We are as such before God.

"And we, though many, throughout the earth, we are one body in this one Lord."

It is important for every individual to have the freedom to practice his or her own religion. This is because every person is uniquely on his or her own path to oneness with the Lord. It is also conceivable that in God's infinite mercy, one may be able to enter the gates of Heaven no matter where one's position on the path—if your heart is pure.

And yet, one must ask, "Why would one willingly choose not to be as close to God as humanly possible?"

Jesus, in entering the world to redeem us from our sins, provided clarity on how to achieve salvation. *Christianity*—Catholicism and the many denominations of Protestantism—*celebrates this most important part, the glory of Jesus Christ as our Lord and Savior.* Meanwhile, Judaism is the root of Christianity. And even Islam, which branches off from the major tenets of Christianity, accepts Jesus as one of its greatest prophets and includes "The Sermon on the Mount" in the Qur'an. Thus, whenever these religions pray in Truth, I believe, they pray to the same God.

The question each individual must answer in choosing their faith is the same: "How close to God do I want to be?" For some, it means going to a different church within the same denomination. For others, it is a revelation of God's Truth that draws them to convert to another faith. *Seek and ye shall find. Ask and it shall be answered.*

Why would you choose not to be closer to God? *Salvation is only available through God's grace—which is forgiveness—and the exercise of your free will matters.*

Chapter 44

Are You Ready?

We all must ask *ourselves* the question: *"Am I ready?"*

"Am I ready to die and meet my Lord Jesus Christ?" We may not be, but how can we prepare our hearts? *We pray.*

Several years ago Pope John Paul II visited St. Louis, Missouri. When he addressed thousands of youth he asked, "Are you ready?" They did not understand. He asked again, "Are you ready?" Still they did not understand.

It was as if he was trying to tell them that the world they live in is a world that does not believe what they believe. They would be told to choose between evils, even when they really have another choice—love. *When asking them rhetorically, "Are you ready?" he might have also asked them, "Will you reject the world of selfishness?"*

The challenges in our lives are not insignificant, but are you ready to accept these burdens fully? In God's love? *It is only in love that you will find "His burden is light, His yoke easy."*

We can choose to live our lives in blissful ignorance, but we know better. The news is filled with stories of people suffering all kinds of tragedies. "Are these things in store for me or someone in my family? Am I ready?" We must ask ourselves.

Life is not simply a joyous walk from birth to death. At every turn, suffering is part of our journey. *It is only when we come to realize this integrated relationship between pain and joy, love and compassion—by divine intent—that we can find peace knowing that we, too, one day must suffer.*

And peace is what we find when we accept our cross, which requires us "to give until it hurts."

Do you see the yoke of your life as the opportunity to fulfill joy? Do you see opportunities to empty yourself of selfishness and sin as opportunities to give until it hurts?

Joy—the ever-present, overflowing, and life-giving joy—is the reward for being ready.

Are you ready? It is a question of our time—and of every man and woman's lifetime.

Chapter 45

Believing In God and Preparing for Eternal Life

If you believe in God, temporal life becomes a preparation for eternal life. When Pope John Paul II asked youthful believers in St. Louis, "Are you ready?" He might also have asked them, "Do you believe?" Of course, it is our human nature to say we "believe," even if in our hearts we hope to somehow carry a lesser burden than what God requires.

If you embrace God and believe, in the true sense of the word "embrace," you will use your free will to be ready. You'll be willing to give of yourself, empty yourself of self-pride before God, and embrace the path of joy and suffering, and even death, which leads to eternal life.

Asking believers, "Are you ready?" would be a contradiction if believing were enough. We must act on our beliefs and always act in love.

Chapter 46

The Mystery of Eternal Life

The "mystery of eternal life," or simply the "mystery of life," *is that* God's love is always available to us. But *we can only receive it when we are ready to accept it.*

Have you ever loved someone, someone you really wanted to know that you loved them, and yet, if you were to tell that person it would not be the same? Somehow, the *truthfulness* and *fullness* of that person's love for you would be compromised if they did not find it on their own. This is as God's love for us. He wants us to find Him through our humanly will. He always hopes that we will find Him, to discover his perfect love, but it would not be the same—it could not be the same—if He were simply to tell us without us finding Him. *As winding and trying as it can be, our love for Him can only be made perfect through the use of our free will.*

This is because God's love for us is so great. It cannot be compromised. Just as your love for another can be present but not received, God's love for us is present but not embraced until we accept it.

It is the unconditional emptying of oneself of self-pride and sin and the embracing of God's love that creates the opportunity for eternal life. And it must happen every day. God's eternal love for us is real. It cannot be compromised, but it can be found.

Do you accept it? Do you see how you can be made worthy of His love?

Chapter 47

Fulfilling Our Potential in the Eyes of God

So often we wonder, am I fulfilling my potential? A few years ago, my niece celebrated her graduation into spiritual adulthood. Her parents loved her dearly and she showed them and others great appreciation for the many blessings God had given her. In short, as she received many blessings, she showed much appreciation to God and to others, just as God intended.

But how do you honor such a person? And how do you give a gift of not just reward, but also of love? She received many cards and gifts, but one that she remembered for its meaning:

"Congratulations on your Bat Mitzvah. Everything was so beautiful from the synagogue to the reception following to the warm gathering of friends and family at your home.

As your gift, we have given to you and in your name a total of $100. One-half of this amount you will find enclosed. We hope you will add it to your savings for your trip to Israel.

The other half we have provided to a family in Peru. They have three children. They are a hard-working family. He is a lawyer/teacher by profession, but their country has fallen on hard times and he is out of work. Their youngest child is just a baby. Their savings are now so low that they do not have money for diapers and milk. As a reminder to you and ourselves, we have provided them a gift of $50 in your name.

We learn as children of God that we are not alone. We struggle, but so do others. While great gifts and talents we may have, we are called upon in even greater ways to share them. By helping others, we help ourselves. By loving, we find that we are loved.

May you grow and develop in your knowledge of the world, but *let love be known as your gift and how you will be remembered. It is through the use of knowledge and resources in love and compassion that fulfills our potential in the eyes of God."*

She felt sadness and joy, honor and meaning.

In everything you do, are you fulfilling your potential in the eyes of God?

Chapter 48

Crying (When We Want) to Feel Good

Have you ever heard someone say, "I need a good cry"? Sometimes it is because he or she knows their life is out of balance, sometimes because he or she simply remembered how they felt better after a cry—but usually not why.

Many people enjoy the theatre. They love to be entertained by the twists and turns of the plots because they frequently see in the actors their own lives and the lives around them. And oh, how they love to care for others without helping, feel others' pain without hurting, and give generously to the poor without sacrificing their own time or money. This also allows them to give to a degree they think proper. When it seems extraordinary or inconvenient, they simply turn their heads—because this is the theatre—and they can.

But soon, they find that they live their lives in the same self-loving way. No longer do they care for others without acknowledgment. Soon, every gift is a calculated measurement of return, and they cry more in the theatre than in real life. Tears do not lead to action; tears simply lead to more tears.

Do we live tears of Truth? Or simply cry them in the theatre or at home watching television or a movie? Is it enough to be moved, or must we act?

As Mother Teresa has said, "Give until it hurts." Have you decided to give of yourself? Do you give joyfully until it hurts?

If it does not hurt and we have not given in joy beyond what is comfortable, we may find that our actions have not done any good—for others or for ourselves.

Chapter 49

Saints and Martyrs

To understand and appreciate saints and martyrdom, we must fully embrace our faith and believe in everlasting life. Holy people, from Mother Teresa of Calcutta to Pope John Paul II, exuded joy despite the fact they worked under difficult circumstances. Have you embraced the radicalness of your faith? Do you realize that, you and I, we are ALL called to be saints?

They also knew that their goodness was not of them. Self-pride is a great sin. Pride brought St. Joan of Arc and her King to their knees before St. Joan of Arc understood serving God and doing His will should be her guiding principle. Such faith shows true character.

It is not that "only the good die young," it is that occasionally the good die so that others may live more fully. The good who die are young, old, and in between.

Too often, we hold saints and martyrs in such a special place in our hearts that we stop believing that we can be like them. We stop trying at all because we know we have failed so many times before. And yet, our perfection does not rest in achieving it, but in accepting that we must always pursue it.

There is no shame in doing something right today, even if we have failed before. *Our own perfection is being made stronger when we grow to avoid and resist temptation. We are building trust.*

Saints and martyrs knew the depths of sin. In fact, many of them had to overcome great sins on the path to holiness. It is this understanding of the depths of sin that allowed them to be patient with others—the same patience that God extended to them *and extends to you.*

Chapter 50

Miracles and Revelations

Have you thought of the little miracles in your life today? How many times have you shrugged off an occurrence as a coincidence when, in reality, it was much more profound? When you go before the gates of heaven and ask God, "Why did you forsake me?" He may very well respond, "Didn't you notice all of the signs I sent to you? Did I need to stamp them on your forehead? And when you did notice, why didn't you bother to remember?"

Miracles are all around us if we open our eyes and minds. And revelations are offered to our hearts like a mother offers milk to a baby. However, one of the human conditions is to forget; so we must take great pains to remember. One suggestion I have is to create a list of the miracles and revelations that have occurred in your own life. I have given examples in the addendum to this book and offer the blank pages that follow to begin your own.

We must always be slow in attributing without doubt that an occurrence is a miracle or that a revelation is from God. Revelations can have as their source God, man, or the devil, and miracles may result from man's will allowed by God, so we must be careful in our attribution, even if we record them to help us remember. *The Truth of miracles and revelations can only be known over time.*

Despite this caveat, if you remember real-life examples of God's love it will help you live a life of faith.

Chapter 51

Going to Church, Synagogue, or Mosque

Have you ever wondered why we go to church, synagogue, or mosque? Especially since the readings, homilies, and sermons begin to repeat themselves? Our human condition is to forget—so we constantly need reminding.

The Ten Commandments were handed down to Moses in stone. It may be because if Moses had come down from the mountain *without* them written in stone, there would have been several different versions by the next day!

This also may help explain why there are services at church, synagogue, or mosque. The words written and read, which we would otherwise forget, and the expansion on those words in a timely fashion for that day and in that community, is worth hearing. *God did not send the Holy Spirit to be with one individual or a small group of people—the Holy Spirit is within and among all of us and will guide us if we choose to listen to His voice.* Like a radio station that broadcasts to the world—are you listening?

My Dad loved to talk about his father, "Grandpa," and one of the things he told me was that Grandpa used to say, "You need to go to church every week. Every now and then you will hear a kernel of Truth that you can really use." He was so right.

Some people will even say they don't need to go to church because God is everywhere—so they don't need to go to church to be in his presence. However, just as the Holy Spirit has not been completely conveyed to me, it has not been completely conveyed to you—even now. And even when we learn important things, we must be reminded. *We must continuously talk to one another and attend services to be reminded of the things we have already learned, but also to learn more.*

Spiritual nourishment does and should come from each other—*but it can be consistently profound coming from the divinely inspired and spiritually holy, the clergy. In the Holy Eucharist,* where bread and wine is transformed into the body and blood of Christ—*the message of God's love is perfected at every service—regardless of the scripture chosen or the words used to expand on it.* This is even more reason, and the most important one, for going to church.

Are you spiritually malnourished?

Chapter 52

Statues, Icons, and Relics

Centuries ago, God taught us through Moses and the Ten Commandments not to put any other god before Him. Some think that Catholics and others have been caught in this snare, especially when they see statues, icons, and relics of the Virgin Mary or the saints. But this is not the case if one lives in Truth.

Catholics living God's Word see and use these items as a means of reminding themselves of God's glory. They pray on their knees because of the humility it requires of them to do so; the same humility required to empty ourselves of our self-pride before God. The Holy Spirit is present with or without these items, but conversion can be more profound in their presence because of their unique ability to remind us of God's love. This is similar to remembering a deceased father or mother or loved one more deeply in the presence of their graves, photos or videos, or life belongings. It is not necessary in order to remember their love or appreciate the impact they had on your life, but somehow it is more profound. Catholics also know that the *saints have achieved a special place in heaven and can help intercede on their behalf before God. Statues, icons, and relics of the saints remind us of their holiness and ability to overcome sin, the same hope we have for ourselves.*

God is always the source of good and the one who Catholics worship—even if they ask for His help through the intercession of the Virgin Mary or the saints.

And saints remind us that we, too, can overcome sin and share in God's glory. *Goodness is available to anyone willing to accept it.* Learning from the examples of the saints, such as St. Thérèse of the Child Jesus or St. Paul, we have an opportunity anew to become one with God the Father, God the Son, and God the Holy Spirit.

It is not what statues, icons, or relics are on their face—it is how they remind us of our potential and change our hearts that matters.

Chapter 53

Good Deeds

A boy asked his father, "Daddy, what are good deeds?"

"Good deeds are things we do to help other people," said his father. "They include big and small things, from opening the door for someone to working a lifetime making things better for others. *When we do these things, we do not seek recognition, but rather, we do these things to serve one another as Jesus taught us. In our hearts, we know when we do good things to seek recognition—we receive our thanks here on earth. But in serving one another, our actions should always be done without regard to personal earthly recognition. Our reward is in heaven.*"

"Is that why we do good deeds in private?"

"Yes. *One does not have to do a good deed in private, but a good deed done in private is always rewarded in heaven,*" said his father. *"For other good deeds, such as those that gently remind others of their own obligation to help others, God knows if your heart is in it for those to be helped or for your own recognition here on earth.* Do not be concerned about what others might say—do your good deeds and be pure of heart. It would please God."

Chapter 54

Eternal Damnation

Over the course of his lifetime, a man realized that he had hurt many people. On some occasions, he did so inadvertently; he was so focused on what he was doing that he denied love to his family and his friends. On other occasions, he does not know why, he ignored those in need around him—the frenzied co-worker who needed a friend, the motorist who needed help, or the homeless person on the street.

But how could he fix the wrong he had done? Is it possible to correct so many wrongs done over the course of a lifetime? Are there wrongs so great that they cannot be overcome?

His answer came in a single sentence: "Only you can choose eternal damnation."*

No matter the offense, eternal damnation can only occur if you choose it. It is not for the offended to judge, although they will. It is not for the public to ridicule with disdain, although they might. And even behind bars, it is not steel and cement that confine—*it is the soul of the accused that confines.*

One must ask for God's forgiveness, forgive his persecutors (even if he or she is innocent), and accept God's peace.

And it takes time.

Escaping damnation, as the man learned, begins with a simple decision to ask for forgiveness. But he had to make it. *And forgiveness, although made possible by Jesus dying on the cross for us, cannot be received* (even after we ask for it, because remember, we also made the decision to commit sin) *until it is granted.* In a similar way, forgiveness from those he has hurt

---

* Based on a weekly address by Pope John Paul II as reported by *The Catholic News and Herald.*

cannot be received until they have reconciled their painful condition with God. This is part of why *we must avoid the greatest depths of sin.* It is a sort of reverse pain (or purgatory) for the guilty who have hurt others, but it is real. When we receive forgiveness from those we have hurt, it can help us in our reconciliation with God. As an example, when we die and request salvation, *prayers from others or the lack of prayers from others can help or leave more difficult our path to eternal salvation.*

God offers us peace—eternal peace. But we must choose to accept it. *Even in its slowest form of coming,* such as asking forgiveness for the most heinous of sin and patiently offering penance, *it is infinitely better than suffering eternal damnation.*

Chapter 55

Embracing Goodness

How many times in your life have you witnessed the goodness of another only to find yourself in a strange way feeling upset, or even jealous? Instead, we should embrace goodness wherever it is, in our friends *and* in our enemies, because it is always from the love of God.

Have we forgotten that God sheds his love on *all* his children, whomever they are? Are we upset that it is shared even with our enemies? Instead of disdaining God's love in our enemies, *we should embrace goodness—wherever it is—all we must do is avoid our own threshold of temptation.*

For those who seem to be good all the time, do we resent their goodness because of our own shortcomings? Rather than act in a way to encourage them to be more like us, shouldn't we simply give thanks for their goodness and ask God to help us be more like them?

Embracing goodness is simply embracing God's love. And we should forgive as we hope to be forgiven—even if it means forgiving someone who has hurt you—even if it means forgiving someone who has hurt someone you love.

We should empty ourselves of self-pride and let go of the guilt of our own shortcomings and love others as Jesus loved us. *God not only communicates directly with us, but also through His love of another.*

Chapter 56

Humor

Does God have a sense of humor? I believe the answer is a resounding, *"Yes!" This is because all of the ways that God communicates to our hearts are from Him—including laughter. But the difference between His humor and man's humor is that His humor is always out of goodness—never out of meanness.*

Have you ever noticed that you learn things about yourself when you hear somebody else talk about you? It is like this with humor. You or I have a perception of ourselves that is one-sided, based on our perceptions of ourselves in multiple experiences, but it is still just one view. *Through humor, others help us learn more about ourselves, telling us of whom they see—not just who we think we are.*

My oldest daughter, Laura, who has a great sense of humor, sat at our kitchen table eating breakfast with me when she was two years old. I was reading the newspaper when soon I noticed that she kept making an intense frown with wrinkled eyebrows. She would wrinkle her eyebrows and laugh, and then wrinkle her eyebrows and laugh. I couldn't figure out what she was doing until I realized she was mimicking me!

What a wonderful gift humor can be to help us take ourselves less seriously.

Humor should not be mean. It should not be hurtful. It should always be in love. For those trying to make others laugh, it should always be in love to help others love and encourage love, and not embarrass for the sake of being mean.

The more you laugh at silly things or nonsense, the more you will share the innocence of a child's love of another. For what can be more fun than the laugh of a child? You can be sure that Mary and Joseph laughed with Jesus when He learned to walk and talk—*because the laughter of a child is an expression of pure love.* And to know God is to laugh with Him on the journey to find His love.

Chapter 57

Politics and Labels

Many years ago, there was a man who was very concerned about heaven and earth—concerned about how he was supposed to live his life on earth so he could enter heaven. He wondered, "Should I participate in the political system or abstain and simply remain untarnished by the inevitable harshness of politics? At first, he thought he could preserve his neutrality, but then he realized that once he knew anything about the issues, "watching" would be a decision just as much as "doing." He then asked himself, how should I participate?

He prayed for guidance. It did not come to him through a thunderbolt, although it could. It did not come to him through a voice in the night, although that could happen as well. No, he knew in his heart after a period of peaceful solitude.

God is not a Republican or a Democrat. And neither Democrats nor Republicans have a corner on heaven. Holiness is not predetermined and cannot be determined by a single decision. In fact, it is determined by countless acts every day. And living a life of faith leads to consistency in all of our actions.

But how should he participate? With whom? And when?

Love is present everywhere—and will grow if we foster it. And the question is not which party is right; both can be right and wrong. The decisions for whether, how and when to participate ought to be founded in love.

As an example, *both parties must strive to show the greatest love. This "greatest" love requires love for the defenseless—from the least fortunate among us, such as the poor and the oppressed, to those who are conceived but still unborn.* And it is when we make these decisions that we move closer to or move farther away from God. While God is infinitely patient, *whenever we make decisions to reject His love we make more difficult our own salvation. This is especially the case when we enable or encourage others to reject His love.* It deepens the challenge of our own salvation.

People choose labels all the time to hide their own shortcomings. This is wrong. *And some people support policies out of tradition even though they no longer help.* This, too, is wrong. Similarly, people choose parties as if it is the only decision they will need to make, even though it is only one of many decisions.

Honoring God and being thankful for the wonderful gift of life (for ourselves and others) comes first. Treating others the way we want to be treated comes second. And if done right, we will also follow Jesus' Great Commandment, "to love others as I have loved you." It is then that we will have participated in a political system according to God's will.

Chapter 58

History

"How is history unfolded?" If God exists, aren't we just playing out something that is predetermined?"

These are questions asked by many people who wonder in their hearts how it is that history unfolds. Again, as Pope John Paul II said, *"History is not a meaningless series of events, but is the path humanity travels toward God."**

And history matters. Just as God shared with man the Ten Commandments at a certain point in time, they did not exist on earth before then. Just as Jesus' death and then resurrection are the fulfillment and the very point of strength in the Christian faith, this fulfillment did not exist on earth before it happened.

Similarly, we live our lives seeking to do God's will, avoiding it, or directly challenging it, and history is the result of these actions on the path to find God.

In God's infinite mercy, we are not alone on our path to find Him. He is always with us. We will find him if we seek Him. But He can be absent in our wills or the wills of others. *This is perhaps the most confusing aspect of history: each individual has the capacity to choose God's will or reject it.* It is not God's will that everything that happens to you should happen. However, God does promise that He will always give you the strength you need to handle whatever life gives you—if you only ask Him. And, His strength will prevail if you choose Him.

---

* Pope John Paul II weekly address as reported by *The Catholic News and Herald.*

In this way, history is not predetermined. History is a result of the intertwining of man's free will and God's will. And we cannot know exactly the balance until we join Him in heaven.

God strengthens and protects the few who choose Him, but he also strengthens and protects the masses if they choose Him as well.

A man loses his job. A woman mourns the death of one of her children. A family suffers as it watches one of its loved ones choose a life of drugs and addiction. Are these occurrences the result of man's will or God's? We cannot know for sure, but we can know that God will give us the strength to handle whatever happens. *And our will matters.*

The life of the Virgin Mary serves as a beacon of hope for mankind. Born without sin, the first since Eve, *she chose to live her life according to God's will—unlike Eve. We can do the same.*

History unfolds with the exercise of our free wills. Mary lived her life without sin and was honored by her assumption into heaven and coronation as the Queen of Heaven. These things did not always exist. They happened during the course of history as a result of her free will that was consistent with God's will.

Jesus Christ, very different from Mary because He was God, lived his life as a man, and *through the exercise of his free will* in the face of pain, humiliation, and ultimately death, *gave us freedom to cleanse ourselves from sin.* These things happened as a result of Jesus' free will. *And we, too, must choose.* The Holy Spirit is all around us—as is evil. *And our decisions will change the course of history.*

If we simply expect God to do His will, it is likely we will find ourselves in greater darkness as others express their free will. If we ask for His help and seek guidance every day through prayer, we will have the opportunity to live His will and improve the course of history.

Chapter 59

Timelessness in Heaven

Many times I have witnessed people lose focus on the things that are most important to them—seemingly only to lose everything they have previously gained. It is as if the things they do *today* affect even the things they did *yesterday*. While we think of the things on earth as a chronological sequence of events, in heaven, where time does not exist as on earth, events occur in what is best described as an *"ever-present now."* The past, present, and future occur in the present tense.

An example of this is when a child falls and scrapes his knee. As adults observing the fall, we know this is just a small event in life. Perhaps he will learn not to run so fast or to be more careful. But he will survive. In fact, we know this is just one part of his life. This is similar for God. Even though we may only see the immediate pain and suffering of a particular moment, the "scraped knee," he knows the future at the same time and knows the good that can come from the moment, even if he allows us to co-author history to determine when and how joy will overcome pain and suffering—and when and how good will overcome evil.

The question for us is will we help to overcome evil and pain and suffering sooner or later—or will we choose to help at all? God has a plan for you and me. Are we even looking for it? Do we know it's real?

The concept of timelessness in heaven is important because we can begin to understand how God urges us to change our lives or to do something to avoid tragedy or to gain success: He already knows the outcome and is urging us to change our ways to change the outcome.

The most beautiful and simple example of the timelessness in heaven is Jesus' statement, *"I am."*

Sometimes, when we experience success after a sequence of events, we begin to repeat a sequence as if the sequence is the source of our success. When God is absent from our hearts, this can only be described as superstition. And yet, God is infinitely creative just as we must be creative in finding him, and wants us to listen with our hearts. This is the case in doing holy activities in repetition, such as going to mass or praying the rosary. (Remember, these activities are very different from superstition because they share in, and are in, the presence of God in heaven.) God is also present when we do the things of everyday life at peace. How surprised we are when we learn He wants us to do something we have never done before!

In the church, saints are not determined until well after their deaths. This is not just to allow more time to unveil the impact they have had, *but to know more fully what heaven has always known—everything they have ever thought, said, done, or failed to do.* It is also in this fuller understanding of who they were on earth that we can understand the good graces they have received from God. *It is in this way that we measure a man or woman by their many actions, and especially their closing chapter on earth, to determine who they were on earth and who they are in heaven.* The final proof of sainthood is two miracles on earth that occur as a result of their intercession. It is a summation of their standing in heaven that is only possible because of their love of God and the love they have gained from Him.

By gaining some understanding of the timelessness in heaven, we also learn how the last chapter of life is to be closed on earth. *In order for His will to be done, our lives must be allowed to be closed by God.* It is the only way to know with certainty that He has no more plans for us on earth.

On earth, we can directly affect the course of history—as co-authored with God. *In heaven, in communion with the saints, we can only do good on earth through intercession with God as a result of prayers—prayers from souls still on earth as well as prayers from souls in heaven.*

Our actions on earth *always* affect who we are in heaven. And purgatory after death allows us to overcome our sins to enter heaven. It is *on earth* that we can ask for forgiveness of our sins and overcome our faults as a direct result of prayers *and* action*s*. In death and *in everlasting life* after life on earth, we will *only* have *prayers*.

Chapter 60

Demons, Addictions, and the Devil

Many people take a very nonchalant attitude towards evil. They think, "Are there really people who would challenge God's goodness? Are there demons? Can addictions be traced to the desires of the devil?"

They think they can do anything, try anything, and still make a decision at a later time on whether to continue or to stop. They have no idea about the power of evil.

In conversation with a priest at my parish, the power of evil became more apparent to me. He said it takes a great love of God for someone to withstand the danger of performing an exorcism—extracting the presence of demons or the devil from man. Even though a priest, he would not attempt one. He explained that only someone who is highly trained should even attempt one. In a similar manner, you would not ask your family doctor to do the work of a specialized surgeon.

Great evil is a danger for all souls, even a parish priest. And small evils in our hearts can become great evils if we let them grow.

As proof of evil's great power, remember Lucipher was not just "any" angel that decided to challenge God. Lucipher was God's top angel, the No. 2 in command in doing good when he was overcome by temptation. Don't underestimate the power of evil. The dangers of evil must be acknowledged, even if just to recognize the potential for great evil and avoid temptation and its all too often sin.

As Jesus taught us, "Lead us not unto temptation but deliver us from evil."

Do you see how prayer, especially the Lord's Prayer, can help protect us from evil? Including small evils in our hearts?

Chapter 61

Where Was God?

"Where was God?" A newspaper columnist asked this question after the tragic deaths of a young mother and a young driver in a traffic accident. In this accident, the young driver crossed the median and struck the young mother's car head-on—killing her as well as himself.

I would ask, *"Where was I? Where were you? Where were we?"*

God provided us free will. It is conceivable that any one of us could have helped him or her or to keep them from harm.

In an instant, the use of our free will, such as the young driver's, can put us in a position to cause others or ourselves great harm.

Where were we in reaching out to this young man to help him respect his free will, live more cautiously, and protect himself and others?

Where were we in asking for God's intervention to protect innocent people from accidental harm?

We cannot understand the consequences of such an accident, and thus we cannot know why God allowed this accident to happen. But we can be comforted in knowing that God will not send us more than we can handle. We also know He is a just God, a merciful God, and a loving God. And in an earthly sense, even though God is perfect, our time on earth can never be perfect because He gave us and others free will.

In heaven, where our lives are always in the present, God already knows the consequences of what we do and how we can overcome the consequences of what we do—to become stronger—even whether and when we will. Perhaps this is how God is able to allow us to endure the things on earth we find so painful.

Our obligation is to pray and to use our free will to help reduce the causes of such accidents. Prayer and action both matter.

Chapter 62

Emptying Oneself and Forgiveness

Sin separates us from God. In order to become closer to God, we must empty ourselves of everything that separates us from Him, including the evil in our hearts. As Jesus said, "All these evils come from within." (Mark 7:23) To reunite with Him, we must empty ourselves of sin and the thoughts of sin in order to receive His forgiveness.

And the emptying of ourselves and forgiveness are connected. At the high point of the Mass, we relive Jesus' giving his body, the bread of life, to us. We also relive Jesus' emptying himself of living in our weakness by giving his blood as a new covenant so that our sins may be forgiven. *When He emptied himself of the potential for sin He made it possible for our shackles to sin to be broken. When He rose from the dead, our sins were forgiven.*

The physical emptying of oneself, such as through fasting and prayer, is particularly helpful in becoming spiritually closer to God. This is important before and during Mass. And offerings of physical comfort at any point in our day can also bring us closer to God.

Offerings of doing your best to do God's will, whether caring for a sick child or battling an illness, can also empty ourselves and bring us closer to God. *However, we must not confuse exhaustion at these activities with how God wants us to empty ourselves. Unless these things are done without self-pride, selfishness, or sin, one is not "empty." It is when we are empty as Jesus emptied himself for us that we share in God's infinite strength.*

When empty, you will be able to ask for God's forgiveness without reservation. You will also be very attentive to His will—even to the point of knowing when God lives within you.

And it is when your selfish will is broken that you can accept peace—the peace He offered to us at the Last Supper so many years ago.

Chapter 63

Knowing All Things
and Comprehending All Mysteries

If you know all things and comprehend all mysteries but do not love God, your family, your neighbors, your enemies, and yourself—what difference does it make?

It's like a man who says, "Pay attention to what I say and not what I do." At first, it may seem that his knowledge will be rewarded with great treasures in heaven, *but if he forgets or chooses not to love those he has learned he must, it is as if he has learned nothing.*

How many times have your good intentions been misdirected because you *forgot* to love God and love your neighbor as yourself—especially when you have forgotten to serve others as Jesus did for us?

Or how many times have you *chosen* not to love God and your neighbor as yourself—even though you know you must?

By acting only in love, you will change the very things you do.

Chapter 64

Coming Home

How many times have you been lost in your life?

In a physical sense, we have all experienced this. *In a spiritual sense, we have all experienced this as well. Brothers, sisters, in-laws, friends, strangers, even enemies, they all need love when they are lost, just as we need it from them when we are lost.*

My mother used to say, "If you want to find out how much trouble you can have in your life, just stop going to church." When we drop away from God in our everyday affairs, we find that peace is the very thing we lose—in our hearts, in our homes, and in our communities.

"Coming home" simply means returning to your faith in God. And it is not a sign of weakness. It takes great strength to turn away from selfishness and self-pride and empty yourself of your own will to embrace God's love—even though you will find His burden is light, His yolk is easy.

We must simply turn our backs to those things that separate us from God's love—and seek and do God's will.

You will know when you are home because your heart will overflow with simple joy, despite your many burdens. Your path will be made clear despite life's many choices. And anxiety will leave you, even though your responsibilities may increase.

At work, at home, or at play, why would you wait? Come home—come back to your faith in God—come back to church.

Chapter 65

The Meek Who Do God's Will
Shall Inherit the Earth

A young man was about to leave home when he read in the Bible that it is easier for a camel to pass through the eye of a needle than a rich man to enter the gates of heaven. He also read how the meek shall inherit the earth. He thought, "Does this mean a man should forego wealth and power to save his soul?"

From his brief life experience, he knew that wealth did not come easily, but he also knew it was difficult to keep. He also found being poor was easy to achieve, but it was a difficult way to live. When poor, he also found it was difficult to give to others because he was already in a deficit for meeting his own needs.

So how can one inherit the earth, especially if one is meek? And how can he help others if he, too, is weak?

He discovered that being "meek" is not "weak." Tremendous strength is harbored in the hearts of those who struggle. If anything, the hunger they feel is sought by the wealthy—for good and evil purposes.

The meek who shall inherit the earth are those who turn away from selfishness and self-love. It is in this state that we are "poor in spirit." When we give thanks and praise to God and love others as ourselves, loving as Jesus loved us, we find that we are doing God's will. Occasionally His will will surprise us, but we still embrace it. When it is the more difficult path, we still follow it.

The man grew in faith, hope, and love and God honored him with abundance. *In return, as a man to whom much is given, he gave to others with an open heart—and always from the first fruits and not the last.*

His strength grew like a man who in poverty has found strength despite the absence of earthly treasures. *His wealth grew when his wealth did not matter to him, and he gave freely.*

He tended to the garden of labor, not for the sake of wealth, but in order to give. And he understood how the meek shall inherit the earth.

Chapter 66

The Gift of Life

Deep in our hearts, we know life is a gift. And life certainly did not come from nothing. It comes from that which has always been—God.

As parents, or as friends and relatives of newborn mothers, we see and know firsthand that life is a gift—although undeserving, we are bestowed a gift to nurture and to love. And just as we must take care of the gifts given to us by friends, we must take care of the gift of life given to us by God.

The gift of life for man includes the gift of free will. Even though *we cannot require our neighbor to love us, we can hope that they will choose to love us, and we can love them.*

We can also defend God's will for us to respect the gift of life by protecting the young and the unborn, as well as the old and the disabled—to help families choose life. *We must do this to protect ourselves and others from temptation*, even if ultimately the choice on whether to accept God's gift of life is one each mother and father, son and daughter, must make.

For those who say they believe in God but choose to reject His gift of life, I would ask three questions: 1) "If God exists, do you think we can choose abortion and euthanasia without eliminating the opportunity for His will to be done?"; 2) "Does eliminating the opportunity for His will to be done make His divine plan more difficult?"; and, 3) "Are there consequences for challenging His will?"

God wants us to choose life—to choose the path that respects life. In its most fundamental form, we must respect the dignity of life, no matter its stage of development or deterioration. *When we choose life we allow God's will to be done as He intended.*

Chapter 67

Sexual Relations

For many young men and women, their minds wander frequently to the pursuit of sexual pleasure. Harmless it seems, and yet in pandering to the thoughts of sexual relations outside of Holy Matrimony, they create a distance between themselves and God.

They have yet to learn that a man and a woman drawn together by the strength of love, strength of free will, and the strength of character, pierce the very thing they wish to become if their act of love is outside of God's will. In such an act, shallowness and emptiness await them and the freedom they have gained by the giving of themselves to each other is lost.

In seeking pleasure without God's love, they will find that it cannot satisfy. *Only pleasure found in God's love can satisfy.*

On earth, we chase ecstasy in its many forms, in adulterous affairs, in masturbation, in drugs and the sensations of escape, but the most heavenly ecstasy on earth can only come through a Holy union here on earth—a holy union through Holy Matrimony, Holy Orders, or living a holy single life in harmony with God's will. It satisfies and grows in satisfaction. At its core, it requires the giving of oneself consistent with God's will, such as emptying ourselves of selfishness and self-pride, which in return fills us with overflowing love.

Seeking near heavenly experiences on earth without holiness leads to emptiness and loneliness. Instead, we should seek holiness and its resulting fullness and joy. A man and a woman living sacred lives in Holy Matrimony, men and women living with honor in religious life, or holy singles, meet these tests.

It is worth waiting for and seeking.

Chapter 68

Self-Esteem

A long time ago I knew a girl whose parents no longer loved each other and got divorced. Before the divorce and especially after, she saw the little differences between her mother and father become larger and larger.

As she got older, and without being able to fully understand how it had impacted her self-esteem, she vowed not to make the same mistakes as her mother. However, in her mind, whenever she met boys, she wondered if any relationship between a man and a woman could last. She also knew from watching the experience of her mother that being alone could be very sad.

Soon, she longed for a boy in her life. But how could she interest a boy? *Instead of valuing herself as a temple, she decided to offer her body in the pursuit of love. This 'bodily' pursuit of love was self-fulfilling because there are always boys interested in a physical relationship, even if it is absent of love.* Soon, she found herself in a physical relationship with a boy. He said, "I love you," but it was not of God's love.

The very thing she vowed to avoid occurred in her life. The boy she so longed to have took her for granted. They fought and she cried, and soon she was alone.

Years later, she realized that somehow she had viewed herself at the time as not being worthy of love. She knew that God had promised her love, just as He had promised her mother love, but she had not trusted Him. Feeling the absence of love, and not knowing how to address it, she took whatever love she could find.

Now, seeing herself having taken a substitute for the real thing, she learned it was a lack of self-esteem, a belief that she was not worthy of God's love, that led her to seek and give in to boys too weak to say "no."

A healthy form of believing we are "not worthy," such as when we say it at Mass, is offered only in humility, and never in the context of promoting one's flesh to another, and is the very moment when it is possible for us to be made worthy of God's love.

It is when we are absent of self-love, and acknowledge our weakness without Him, that we enable our self-esteem to soar—through the goodness of the Lord. Through Him, with Him, in Him, in the unity of the Holy Spirit, we are able to soar on the wings of the goodness of the Lord.

After much suffering, greater than if she had stayed the course of a virgin, she discovered that great love is always available to all who love Him first. With this love embedded in her being, her self-esteem soared and she found it easy to be treated with dignity and respect.

She found the love she had always longed for, and along the way, learned that she had always been loved.

Chapter 69

Humility

Humility should be the foundation of the morning, afternoon, and evening of our lives. It is not without joy, for it is truly joyous to live. It is not without sorrow, for we shall surely meet sorrow on the path of history. But it is also with thunderous glory that we shall one day see "our" accomplishments, not simply as a betterment of mankind, but as a glorification of God.

When you have humility, you laugh with others at your own imperfections. When you have humility, you are incapable of thinking how much "I have accomplished," but rather, you think of how much you have been blessed and helped by others. In all things, your heart is open to goodness, whether from friend or foe. Like a child, you understand without pretensions, often without the knowledge of experience.

In humility, God is present in our hearts. Have you experienced and will you experience all things—the beginning, middle, and end of your life—with humility? With a humble and contrite heart? With God living in your heart? *It is His will and as God intended.*

Chapter 70

National and International
Life Changing Events

Throughout history, there have been thousands, if not millions, of significant events. However, occasionally, there are events that dwarf even those things that happened before and after them. *For a nation, I call them "national life-changing events." They always have an element of personal significance, especially for those directly involved, but they differ because they are shared by the nation.* Recent examples for America in the last half-century include the shooting of John F. Kennedy, Jr., where a nation wept; the walking of a man on the moon, where a nation rejoiced; the ending of the Vietnam War, where a nation mended its wounds; and the Persian Gulf War, where hundreds of thousands of families prayed as loved ones left for the battlefield, first in Desert Shield, and then gave thanks in the triumph of Desert Storm. *In every instance, these events shaped those directly involved as well as those who witnessed it from afar.*

As in personal life-changing events, they impacted a nation in ways we had not experienced before. In countless ways, people were changed. *In each event, prayer and God's response, in combination with man's will, intertwined to make history. We honestly did not know what to expect—and yet we shared in its experience.*

In the last decade, the terrorist attacks on the World Trade Center in New York, the Pentagon, and the hijacked plane that crashed in Pennsylvania represent a new national and international life-changing event. As with other national life-changing events, most of us remember where we were, how we found out, and even what we thought. Although it was a life-changing event for the thousands directly involved, it was a national and international life-changing event for the hundreds of millions who watched and listened from afar.

We cannot know yet the full impact of this recent national and international life-changing event, but like individual life-changing events, it will result in a "new normal." And we will be changed in immeasurable ways—many impacts only to be known years later.

Addendum

Remembering Miracles and Revelations

Over the course of a lifetime there are thousands, even millions of miracles that you will see, hear, feel, taste, or smell—or just know. *There are those that happen without our involvement, like the rising and setting of the sun, but also those that happen as a result of our own heartfelt prayer.*

For me, I will begin with the first miracle I can remember. At the age of five, I was on a family vacation at a park where as kids we laughingly ran along a path near a waterfall with rushing water and slippery walls. I slipped and fell through a crack between the hillside and a log railing. I grabbed the bottom log of the railing and hung on for dear life. Three of my siblings were near me and came to my aid. *As I was dangling over the falls, I lost one of my shoes, but miraculously, they pulled me up to safety.* (I still have the remaining shoe.)

Little miracles included the mundane such as doing well on a test when I was not prepared. Another lifesaving miracle for me occurred while driving the Pennsylvania Turnpike in the late fall and getting caught in an early snowstorm. I had watered down my wiper fluid to save money and the windshield wiper line froze in the subfreezing weather. I could not spray my windshield as I drove down the interstate with trucks in front, beside, and behind me. With 20 miles to go to the next exit, my only visibility through the windshield was a spot about the size of a quarter. *Knowing it would be more dangerous to stop on this mountainous interstate than to keep moving, I prayed to God to protect this smallest of visibility—but I also accepted that if he allowed the ice and salt to block my view, I would stop the car on the shoulder.* Miraculously, I traveled the next 20 miles over 40 minutes with only this quarter-sized visibility—even though the rest of the windshield had been covered in salt during the first two miles!

Revelations ranged from the wonderment of a freshly fallen snow and knowing that God was behind this winter wonderland, to understanding that God is real from seeing the impact from the act of prayer and seeing the powerlessness from the absence of prayer. And I learned that prayer requires the emptying of oneself of selfishness and self-pride and accepting God's will, even if you are praying for a specific outcome.

A recent revelation occurred when I was talking to a family friend who sincerely believed that his life on earth could be followed by other lives, perhaps seven or eight lives spanning 500 years, to enable his soul to achieve perfection. *In discussing whether one could "believe" and accept God in a moment, or whether one needs several lifetimes, he understood that if he has a chance to believe in this lifetime, this might be his only chance. I urged him to reconsider his belief; I told him this is his chance.*

In brevity, I will list other examples of miracles and revelations I have experienced, witnessed, or heard about. I encourage you to do the same in the blank pages that follow:

Miracle—My brother's hemorrhaging subsides after days of intense prayer and personal vigil after the accident that takes the lives of three of our sisters and a cousin.

Miracle—My parents and several of my siblings watch in amazement as a picture hanging on a wall in our house slowly falls to the floor before their eyes. This occurred soon after the last accident—almost as if my deceased siblings were saying they were okay and still there, even if for just a little while.

Miracle—With the assistance of intense prayer, one of my brothers' teams wins the state football championship in double-overtime against a bigger and faster team in an unbelievable comeback. *[Although I do not believe sports to be the preferred use of prayer, any time we ask for God's help it brings us closer to Him—as long as we are open to His will.]*

Miracle—My mother-in-law's swelling in her leg subsides after hip surgery when her husband of 40 years prays the rosary for the first time in decades.

Miracle—While writing this book, and after sharing the chapter about our son Philip James' death for a separate book to be published by my parish* the next spring, God gives us another son—Jon Philip Gauthier.

Revelation—Only God is the source of miracles, although saints and others may intercede to remind Him of our faith.

Revelation—We must die to self-pride and selfishness every day. Prayer is the first step to acknowledging God and reducing one's self-centeredness.

Revelation—It is through prayer *and* actions that we show our love of God.

Revelation—Being open to God's will does not mean that we do not want a specific outcome. In fact, the greater the purity of our love, the more likely our requests will be granted.

Miracle—Suffering from a severe sinus infection in the middle of the night and unable to sleep, I remembered Jesus' suffering for our sins and offered up my pain for the sins of others. Immediately, as if to say, 'You're correct, but not worthy of such pain,' the pain went away.

Revelation—Jesus gave us a New Commandment, "to love others as I have loved you." Offer up pain, especially when it consumes you, for the sins of others.

---

* *Threads of Hope: Finding Unity Through Our Stories of Faith*, Written By and For the St. Matthew Church Community. Compiled by Tuesday Trippier, published February 2003.

YOUR MIRACLES AND REVELATIONS:

www.ingramcontent.com/pod-product-compliance
Lightning Source LLC
Chambersburg PA
CBHW071014120626
46546CB00003B/1082